LIBRARY & INFORMATION SCIENCE QUESTION BANK

(For NET/SET/JRF Aspirants & Entrance Examinations of M.Phil/Ph.D/NVS/KVS)

LIBRARY & INFORMATION SCIENCE QUESTION BANK

(For NET/SET/JRF Aspirants & Entrance Examinations of M.Phil/ Ph.D/NVS/KVS)

by

ANAND KUMAR

Librarian

Shri Sharda Sadan Library

Lalganj, Vaishali, Patna (Bihar)

Ess Ess Publications

New Delhi

LIBRARY & INFORMATION SCIENCE QUESTION BANK

(For NET/SET/JRF Aspirants & Entrance Examinations of M.Phil/Ph.D/NVS/KVS)

While extensive effort has gone into ensuring the reliability of information appearing in this book, the publisher makes no warranty, express or implied on the accuracy or reliability of the information, and does not assume and hereby disclaims any liability to any person for any loss or damage caused by errors or omissions in this publication.

This Question Bank is the intellectual work of the author. Resemblance of any question with any of the previous years' question(s) or with any other question bank's question(s) would merely be a coincidence.

ISBN : 978-93-87698-83-3
Price : Rs. 750/-

First Published 2021

Published by:
Ess Ess Publications
4831/24, Ansari Road,
Darya Ganj,
New Delhi-110 002.
INDIA
Phones: 23260807, 41563444
Fax: 41563334
E-mail: info@essessreference.com
www.essessreference.com

Cover Design by *Patch Creative Unit*

Printed and bound in India

Dedicated to

MY LOVING PARENTS

Whose Tireless Efforts and Motivation
Made me able to Write This Book

Contents

Preface

This book is written for the students of library and information science who are preparing for competitive examinations such as NET, SET, JRF, NVS, KVS, and entrance examinations of M.Phil., Ph.D. etc. There are 25 practice sets each containing 60 objectives questions thus making the total of 1500 questions covering all the facets of the discipline. Answers are given at the end of every set for clear understanding and assistance. Effort has been made to include each every aspect of library and information science so as to enable the students/aspirants get comprehensive and clear understanding of the subject so that they can easily crack the entrance/competitive examination they wish to appear for. Although extensive efforts have been made to keep the text error free but if inadvertently something has escaped my attention, I shall welcome the suggestions/corrections. It is Hoped that the book would be a welcome and a valuable addition to the text already available on this theme and would go a long way in helping aspirants clear their respective examinations.

— Anand Kumar

Acknowledgements

I would like to express my gratituide to my teachers Sh. U.M. Thakur, Sh. B. L. Sharma and Sh. Santosh Kumar, my colleague Sh. Arvind Kumar and my friends Sh. Gyanesh Kumar, Sh. Md. Afroz, Sh. Shambhu Sharan and all my friends who inspired me to write this book. Their motivation also helped me in doing a lot of research and I discovered many things I never knew before.

I would also like to thank M/s Ess Ess Publications, who agreed to publish my work, and my parents who helped me a lot in finalizing this book with their support.

– Anand Kumar

Practice Set 1

1. Information is a part of :
   (a) Knowledge (b) Information Processing
   (c) Information Science (d) Information Subject
2. What was the name of National Library of India before Independence?
   (a) Victoria Library
   (b) Raja Ram Mohan Ray Library
   (c) Calcutta Public Library
   (d) Imperial Library
3. Copyright Bulletin is published by :
   (a) INIS (b) UNESCO
   (c) AGRIS (d) MEDLARS
4. Indian Copyright Act was passed in :
   (a) 1990 (b) 1998
   (c) 1995 (d) 1998
5. The Five Laws of library science were enunciated in :
   (a) 1928 (b) 1924
   (c) 1931 (d) 1933
6. The first librarian of National Library, Culcutta was :
   (a) Radhakrishan (b) B.S. Kesavan
   (c) G. Bhattacharya (d) Assadullah Khan
7. The National Science Library is the part of :
   (a) DRDO (b) ISRO
   (c) INFLIBNET (d) NISCAIR

8. Which is the National Library of U.K. :

(a) The British Museum (b) The British Library

(c) Landon Library (d) State Library of UK

9. The Secondary Education Commission (1952-53) was appointed under the chairmanship of :

(a) S.R. Ranganathan (b) B.S. Kesawan

(c) Dr. Mudaliar (d) K.P. Sinha

10. How many sectorial centres of NISSAT are there :

(a) 8 (b) 10

(c) 9 (d) 15

11. Which State First enacted the Public Library Act in India ?

(a) Andhra Pradesh (b) Maharashtra

(c) Tamil Nadu (d) Gujarat

12. Karnataka Public Library Act was enacted in the year:

(a) 1965 (b) 1966

(c) 1968 (d) 1960

13. IASLIC was founded in the year :

(a) 1972 (b) 1961

(c) 1948 (d) 1955

14. DESIDOC was established in :

(a) 1960 (b) 1958

(c) 1948 (d) 1971

15. Khuda Baksh Oriental Library comes under the category of :

(a) Public Library

(b) Special Library

(c) Central Special Library

(d) Central Academic Library

16. Raja Ram Mohan Ray Library foundation (RRRLF) promoted to :
   (a) Public Library (b) School Library
   (c) Special Library (d) University Library
17. Haryana Public Library Act was passed in year :
   (a) 1979 (b) 1975
   (c) 1989 (d) 1986
18. Who Published the "Indian National Bibliography"?
   (a) Central Reference Library, Delhi
   (b) Central Reference Library, Calcutta
   (c) Central Reference Library, Andhra Pradesh
   (d) Central Reference Library, Tamil Nadu
19. "National Index of Translations" is published by :
   (a) DRDO (b) DESIDOC
   (c) INSDOC (d) NISSAT
20. "Indian Books in Print" is an example of :
   (a) Trade Bibliography (b) National Bibliography
   (c) Earth Bibliography (d) Local Bibliography
21. What is Management ?
   (a) Is a management process
   (b) Is a singal process
   (c) Process of Making Collective efforts aimful
   (d) Management is a process
22. What is the meaning of Management ?
   (a) Working one self for the others
   (b) Is a device of taking work from the others
   (c) Both (a) and (b)
   (d) None of these
23. Who was the propounder of "Scientific Theory" of management ?

(a) George R. Tarry (b) Henry La Fountain
(c) F.W. Taylor (d) S. R. Ranganathan

24. What is the full form of 'MBO'?
(a) Management of Objective
(b) Management Bibliography Organisation
(c) Management Biography Organisation
(d) Management Bibliographic Organisation

25. Who propounded the "ACRONYM FOR FUNTIONAL ELEMENTS"?
(a) Henry Fayol (b) Luthar Gullick
(c) Georg R. Tarry (d) S. R. Ranganathan

26. What is the meaning of 'MBO'?
(a) Manage Theory of Function
(b) Manage Through the Objectives
(c) Manage Through the Process
(d) None of these

27. What is the meaning of "Span of Control"?
(a) The Area of the organization be to controlled
(b) Stick Control over the staff by the manager
(c) The Number of Activities that a Manager can effectively manage
(d) None of these

28. Which one in the following is not a type of organizational structure?
(a) Users (b) Departmentation
(c) Staff (d) Managementation

29. In Libraries, Functional Authority is also known as ?
(a) Co-ordinators (b) Co-operation
(c) Helpful (d) None of These

30. The system is made of which of the following :
    (a) By various service
    (b) By various components
    (c) By various objectives
    (d) By various functional
31. What is meant by system analysis ?
    (a) Study and Analysis of the system
    (b) Study of the organization by various method
    (c) Analysis of the components of the system
    (d) None of these
32. 'Binary System' of Number for computers uses only ?
    (a) Six digits (b) Two digits
    (c) Three digits (d) Five digits
33. Which one is the most important part of the computer?
    (a) Monitor (b) UPS
    (c) CPU (d) Printer
34. 'CPU' is a computer is the part of :
    (a) Hardware (b) Software
    (c) Input Device (d) Output Device
35. When Computer was first used in India?
    (a) 1990 (b) 1972
    (c) 1954 (d) 1957
36. Which library in the world developed 'OPAC' Cataloguing system?
    (a) The British Library
    (b) Library of Congress
    (c) American Library Association
    (d) UNESCO
37. When 'ERNET' was started?

(a) In 1980 (b) In 1988
(c) In 1986 (d) In 1996

38. What is the New Name of 'DELNET'?
(a) Developing Library Network
(b) Delhi Library Network
(c) Delivery of Libraries Network
(d) Developed Library Network

39. What is 'DELNET'?
(a) Local network
(b) World Network
(c) Metropolitan Area Network
(d) Wide Network

40. When 'INFLIBNET' was established?
(a) 1980 (b) 1986
(c) 1972 (d) 1973

41. What type of network 'BONET' is?
(a) Local Area Network
(b) World Area Network
(c) Metropolitan Area Network
(d) None of these

42. What is the meaning of 'Research design'?
(a) Working of Research
(b) Planning of Research
(c) Functional of Research
(d) Process of Research

43. Scientific method of Research can be used?
(a) In all disciplines
(b) Only in Science
(c) Only in Social Science
(d) None of these

44. How Hypothesis is verified?
    (a) By Interview (b) By experiments
    (c) By observations (d) By solution

45. What is 'Interview'?
    (a) Analysis of Research (b) Type of Research
    (c) Tool of Research (d) Preservation of Research

46. Who used first the term "Bibliography"?
    (a) Alan Printchard (b) George R Tarry
    (c) A Neelmeghan (d) G Bhattachraya

47. The first library periodicals in India as :
    (a) Library Journal (b) Library Miscallany
    (c) Library Bulletin (d) None of these

48. The first editor of "Modern Librarian" was :
    (a) C.A. Cutter (b) F. Monbray Valte
    (c) H. P. Luhn (d) J. D. Brown

49. 'Modern Librarian' was published first in year :
    (a) 1941 (b) 1939
    (c) 1930 (d) 1950

50. Gazatteer's give information about :
    (a) History of place
    (b) Geographical location of place
    (c) Social custom and practives
    (d) All of the above

51. "Current Awareness Service" was introduced in the year :
    (a) 1950 (b) 1948
    (c) 1960 (d) 1962

52. 'POPSI' is designed by :
    (a) B.S. Kesawan (b) S.R. Ranganathan
    (c) Radhakrishnan (d) G. Bhattacharya

53. Which entry is known as Reference Entry in CCC?
   (a) Cross Reference Entry
   (b) Book Index Entry
   (c) Cross Reference Index Entry
   (d) None of these

54. In 'CC' the Class Number for specials is drived by :
   (a) Analysis (b) Alphabetical device
   (c) Faceted (d) Enumerative

55. Notation has been defined as "a short hand sign" by :
   (a) Richardson (b) Ranganathan
   (c) Cutter (d) Brown

56. In CC the Class Number for Indian Philosophy is :
   (a) R44.7 (b) R44
   (c) R6 (d) R6.44

57. In 'DDC' from divisions were included in :
   (a) 19th edition (b) 15th edition
   (c) 2nd edition (d) 20th edition

58. In 'DDC' Common Isolates are called :
   (a) Relative Index (b) Standard Subdivisions
   (c) Form Divisions (d) Common Subdivision

59. Which main class in 'CC' has facet formula providing four levels of personality facet?
   (a) Chemistry (b) Physics
   (c) Literature (d) Religion

60. What is the basis for the formation of Cutter's Book Number :
   (a) Name of the Author (b) Size of the Book
   (c) Name of the Title (d) Name of the Subject Title

ANSWERS

1. (a)	2. (d)	3. (b)	4. (c)	5. (a)
6. (b)	7. (d)	8. (b)	9. (c)	10. (b)
11. (c)	12. (a)	13. (d)	14. (b)	15. (a)
16. (a)	17. (c)	18. (b)	19. (c)	20. (a)
21. (c)	22. (b)	23. (c)	24. (a)	25. (b)
26. (b)	27. (c)	28. (b)	29. (a)	30. (b)
31. (c)	32. (b)	33. (c)	34. (a)	35. (d)
36. (b)	37. (c)	38. (a)	39. (c)	40. (b)
41. (c)	42. (b)	43. (a)	44. (b)	45. (c)
46. (a)	47. (b)	48. (b)	49. (c)	50. (d)
51. (a)	52. (d)	53. (a)	54. (b)	55. (a)
56. (c)	57. (c)	58. (b)	59. (c)	60. (a)

Practice Set 2

1. What kind of the Notation are used in 'UDC'?
   (a) Pure (b) Mixed
   (c) Enumerative (d) None of these
2. In 'DDC' 19, Table-3 is meant for :
   (a) Subdivisions of Individual Literature
   (b) Standard Subdivision
   (c) Racial Ethics Group
   (d) Language and Literature
3. The concept of common isolate was first introduced by :
   (a) S. R. Ranganathan (b) Melvil Dewey
   (c) C.A. Cutter (d) Henry Fayol
4. How many types of canons in Canons for Array?
   (a) Five (b) Six
   (c) Seven (d) Four
5. "Brain Chamber Diagram" is related with :
   (a) Knowledge of Information
   (b) Concept of Data
   (c) Concept Formation
   (d) None of these
6. The main class 'C' (Physics) is further divided into:
   (a) Compound Class (b) Advance Class
   (c) Low Class (d) Host Class
7. International Communication Format for the exchange of catalogue data :

(a) CIP (b) HTTP
(c) CCF (d) MARC

8. In AACR-II, Standard Number ISBN or ISSN are written :
(a) Tracing Area (b) After the Note Area
(c) Note Section (d) Heading Section

9. According to 'CCC' book written by three Authors. The entry is to be made under :
(a) Third Author (b) Second Author
(c) First Author (d) None of these

10. British museum general catalogue of printed Book is a catalogue :
(a) Title (b) Author
(c) Collaborator (d) Editor

11. Union Catalogue is a form of :
(a) Description Catalogue
(b) Cooperative Catalogue
(c) Centralize Catalogue
(d) Co-operative Catalogue

12. Abstracting and indexing periodicals comes under the category of :
(a) Primary Sources (b) Secondary Sources
(c) Tertiary Sources (d) Communication Sources

13. Indexing and Abstracting services came under which services ?
(a) Current Awareness Services
(b) Select Dessimination Information
(c) Translation Services
(d) Reference Services

14. Social Science Citation Index is published by :

(a) Raja Ram Mohan Ray Library foundation, Calcutta
(b) Institute for Science Information, Philadelphia
(c) University Grant Commission, New Delhi
(d) Developing Library Network, Delhi

15. "Library of Congress" was established in :
(a) 1972 (b) 1800
(c) 1892 (d) 1890

16. The 'BNB' is published by :
(a) British national Bibliographic Division
(b) American Library Association
(c) British Museum Library
(d) The British Library

17. "Raja Ram Mohan Ray Library Foundation" (RRRLF) is a :
(a) Private Institute
(b) Government body
(c) Non-Government Organisation
(d) Public Finance Organisation

18. Who was the first librarian of the "Imperial Library"?
(a) John Macfarlane (b) John Robert
(c) John Woolner (d) G. Bhattacharya

19. Who is known as the Father of Library Movement in U.K. ?
(a) C. A. Cutter (b) Melvil Dewey
(c) Edward Edward's (d) W.H. Philips

20. "Modern Librarian" periodical started by the Punjab Library Association in the year :
(a) 1921 (b) 1937
(c) 1928 (d) 1930

21. In which place DRTC was established in the year 1962?

(a) New Delhi (b) Banglore
(c) Chennai (d) Mumbai

22. Who prepared "Library Development Plan" for India?
(a) S. R. Ranganathan (b) G. Bhattacharya
(c) B.S. Kesvan (d) Assadullah Khan

23. When was Dr. S.R. Ranganathan was appointed as a "National Research Professor of Library Science"?
(a) 1971 (b) 1965
(c) 1962 (d) 1949

24. Which Indian University first started B.Lib.Sc. Course?
(a) Banaras Hindu University
(b) Aligarh Muslim University
(c) Madras University
(d) Punjab University

25. Which Indian university first started M.Lib.Sc. and M. Phil course?
(a) Jawahar Lal Nehru University
(b) Punjab University
(c) University of Delhi
(d) University of Maharashtra

26. Which Commission Recommended 10% of the total College Budget for development of Libraries?
(a) Kothari Committee
(b) Pal Committee
(c) Ranganathan Committee
(d) None of These

27. Where did Dr. S.R. Ranganathan put first his five laws of library science?
(a) Punjab University, Punjab
(b) University of Madras, Madras

(c) Meenakshi College, Annamalainagar
(d) University of Delhi, New Delhi.

28. Number of working days of National Library of India in a year :
(a) 362 Days (b) 365 Days
(c) 360 Days (d) 355 Days

29. Lotka's law deals with :
(a) Scatting of Articles over different journals
(b) Growth of Articles in Journals
(c) Productivity of authors in term of scientific papers
(d) None of these

30. The large volumes of high velocity complex and variable data are termed as :
(a) Small Data (b) Big Data
(c) Linked Data (d) None of these

31. ISO26324:2012 is a standard for
(a) DOI (b) RFID in Librarian
(c) Dublin Core (d) Inter Library Loan

32. The Brown Charging System does not include :
(a) Author Card (b) Title Card
(c) Reader's Ticket (d) Transaction Slip

33. In 'CC' 1 is used for unity, God, World, First in Evolution etc. as a :
(a) Mnemonics
(b) Seminal Mnemonics
(c) Alphabetical Mnemonics
(d) Symbolic Mnemonics

34. 'Facet Publishing' is a division of :
(a) Chartered Institute of Library and Information Professionals

(b) Indian Librarian Association
(c) British Librarian Association
(d) American Library Association

35. What is periodicity of "Annals of Library and Information Studies" published by NISCAIR, India:
(a) Weekly (b) Quarterly
(c) Yearly (d) Monthly

36. Subject entry which refers from the name of a class to its class number is known as :
(a) Class Reference Entry
(b) Main Entry
(c) Class Index Entry
(d) Subject Entry

37. What is the Third Part of Colon Classification?
(a) Theory and books (b) Classic and Sacred Book
(c) Classification Rules (d) None of these

38. Identify the mode of information of the subject "Agriculture of Corn":
(a) Fusion (b) Enumeration
(c) Lumination (d) Diffusion

39. The Number of Successive Characteristics forming the Basis of the derivation from the universe of knowledge is known as ;
(a) Order of a class
(b) Order of a index
(c) Order of a subject index
(d) Order of a class index

40. In which of the following places the Zonal offices of RRRLF are located?
(a) Delhi (b) Mumbai
(c) Both (a) and (b) (d) None of these

41. Which association tagline is "Managing Information":

(a) ASLIB (b) DELNET
(c) INFLIBNET (d) RRRLF

42. When was the international institute of documentation established?

(a) 1939 (b) 1927
(c) 1895 (d) 1952

43. Which organization has introduced the concept of "sister Libraries" for Children and Young adults reading :

(a) UNESCO (b) IFLA
(c) MEDLARS (d) INIS

44. In which year the ISBN allocation office in India shifted from Kolkata to Delhi?

(a) 2011 (b) 2014
(c) 1999 (d) 2005

45. The Shanon-Weaver model of communication consist of :

(a) Nine elements (b) Five elements
(c) Four elements (d) Two elements

46. 'IMPACT' stands for :

(a) Information Making Policy Action
(b) Information Market Policy Action
(c) Informatic Mapping Policy Action
(d) Infotech Matter Policy Action

47. 'Information Service Group' Comes under :

(a) Library Association, USA
(b) Library Association, UK
(c) Library Association, India
(d) Library Association, Canada

48. Who Amongst the Following is regarded as father of 'CYBERNATICS'?
    (a) Novest Weaver (b) George Tarry
    (c) Henry Fayol (d) S.R. Ranganathan

49. The English school of Information Theory was developed by :
    (a) J.D. Brown (b) Allen Kent
    (c) Calin Cherry (d) Neena Brown

50. The terms Information Science is an Advancement of :
    (a) Knowledge Management
    (b) Data Management
    (c) Information
    (d) Documentation

51. MacGraw-Hill International Editions 1988 and Oriental Longman College Catalogue 1987 are the example of :
    (a) Book Catalogue (b) Trade Catalogue
    (c) Library Catalogue (d) Centralize Catalogue

52. The Elementary categories of 'POPSI' are ;
    (a) DEAPPM (b) DEAMP
    (c) DEAPM (d) PMEST

53. In the collation area the size of the Book is preceded by a :
    (a) Colon (b) Semicolon
    (c) Comma (d) Dot

54. The area where the information about the place of publication and date of publication is written is known as :
    (a) Imprint (b) Note section
    (c) Heading section (d) Tracing Section

55. Ranganathan designed method of deriving subject headings for documents :
    (a) Book Index Entry (b) Chain Procedure
    (c) Class Index Entry (d) Subject Entry
56. The birth of 'ILA' took place in the year :
    (a) 1931 (b) 1933
    (c) 1948 (d) 1956
57. The Russian State Library is located in :
    (a) Moscow (b) London
    (c) Paris (d) New York
58. Special Library get their funds from :
    (a) UGC
    (b) Government
    (c) Their parental bodies
    (d) RRLF
59. The budget for a college library is approved by :
    (a) Higher education (b) Library management
    (c) Library authority (d) Library committee
60. What is the Basic Record in the library about each document forming part of its collection :
    (a) Subject Register (b) Accession Register
    (c) List of Catalogue (d) None of these

ANSWERS

1. (b)	2. (a)	3. (b)	4. (d)	5. (c)
6. (a)	7. (d)	8. (b)	9. (c)	10. (b)
11. (d)	12. (b)	13. (a)	14. (b)	15. (b)
16. (a)	17. (b)	18. (a)	19. (c)	20. (d)
21. (b)	22. (a)	23. (c)	24. (b)	25. (c)
26. (a)	27. (c)	28. (a)	29. (c)	30. (a)
31. (a)	32. (d)	33. (b)	34. (a)	35. (b)
36. (c)	37. (b)	38. (c)	39. (a)	40. (c)
41. (a)	42. (c)	43. (b)	44. (a)	45. (c)
46. (b)	47. (b)	48. (a)	49. (c)	50. (d)
51. (b)	52. (c)	53. (b)	54. (a)	55. (b)
56. (b)	57. (a)	58. (c)	59. (d)	60. (b)

Practice Set 3

1. Where was the first library noticed in India :
   (a) Sravasti (b) Savarmati
   (c) Surat (d) Baroda
2. When was information science added to librarianship:
   (a) 1940 (b) 1950
   (c) 1933 (d) 1965
3. 'UAP' stands for :
   (a) Universal Approach Publication
   (b) University Applicable Periodicals
   (c) University Appreciation Period
   (d) Universal Availability Publications
4. Resource Sharing is a part of :
   (a) Library Cess (b) Library Sharing
   (c) Library Cooperation (d) Library Classification
5. When was the American Library Association established ?
   (a) 1940 (b) 1840
   (c) 1876 (d) 1870
6. When was the Library Association established ?
   (a) 1875 (b) 1877
   (c) 1860 (d) 1890
7. When was Special Library Association established ?
   (a) 1909 (b) 1902
   (c) 1948 (d) 1890

8. Which term was coined by Dr. S.R. Ranganathan for mobile libraries?
   (a) Circulate Library (b) Library on Car
   (c) Library on Wheel (d) None of these
9. The Library Day celebrated on :
   (a) 23rd March (b) 5th June
   (c) 10th January (d) 12th August
10. In 'DDC' Education is represented by the number :
   (a) 360 (b) 380
   (c) 370 (d) 350
11. What is meant by e-books?
   (a) Internet book
   (b) Computer book
   (c) Any book on Internet
   (d) Any book available in Electronic Format
12. In AACR-2 edition Statement has to be written in :
   (a) Words (b) Figures
   (c) Indo-Arabic (d) None of these
13. Which one of the following is post-coordinate:
   (a) UNITERM (b) POPSI
   (c) PRECIS (d) All of the above
14. Call Number of a book means :
   (a) Book Number (b) Class Number
   (c) Both (a) and (b) (d) None of these
15. 'COMPENDEX' is an online database for :
   (a) Law (b) Engineering
   (c) Medical (d) Computer Science
16. Patent are which type of Information Sources ?
   (a) Secondary (b) Primary
   (c) Regional (d) Territory

17. To Ascertain Subscription Rate of a Serial, appropriate source is :
    (a) Periodical Directory (b) Dictionary
    (c) Hand Book (d) Encyclopedia
18. Who is regarded as 'Father of Bibliography'?
    (a) S.R. Ranganathan (b) Henry La Fountain
    (c) Conrad Gesner (d) C.A. Cutter
19. 'ETD' database in India is maintained by :
    (a) INFLIBNET (b) DELNET
    (c) Shodhganga (d) None of these
20. Intellectual Property Right is protection given to :
    (a) Patent (b) Trademark
    (c) Copyright (d) All of the above
21. In which year was the Library Act passed in Bihar ?
    (a) 2008 (b) 2006
    (c) 2000 (d) 2005
22. In which year was the Library Act passed in Uttar Pradesh ?
    (a) 2011 (b) 2010
    (c) 2005 (d) 2013
23. In which year was the first publication of the decimal classification scheme?
    (a) 1878 (b) 1876
    (c) 1880 (d) 1904
24. Which year was the First Publication of 'CCC'?
    (a) 1934 (b) 1939
    (c) 1951 (d) 1938
25. Which year was Melvil Dewey Born?
    (a) 1865 (b) 1851
    (c) 1848 (d) 1840

26. Where was Melvil Dewey born?
    (a) America (b) Japan
    (c) London (d) China
27. The American Library Association was founded by :
    (a) J. D. Brown (b) C.A. Cutter
    (c) Milvil Dewey (d) Henry La Fountain
28. What year did the 'Melvil Dewey' die?
    (a) 1925 (b) 1931
    (c) 1885 (d) 1928
29. In which year was the "Nippon Decimal Association" System first published?
    (a) 1956 (b) 1948
    (c) 1890 (d) 1895
30. The "Nippon Decimal Classification" method was published by :
    (a) Canada Library Association
    (b) Japan Library Association
    (c) China Library Association
    (d) Indian Library Association
31. Which of the following can be used to measure the Research output of an Individual?
    (a) H-Index (b) G-Index
    (c) Both (a) and (b) (d) None of these
32. Identify from the following the Silver Halide process used in reprography:
    (a) Developing (b) Exposure
    (c) Rinsing (d) All of the above
33. Identify the type of 'metadata' held by D space for archiving contents:
    (a) Structural (b) Description
    (c) Administrative (d) All of the above

34. Which of the following are 'Special Auxiliary Subdivisions' of DVC?

(a) Apostrophe (b) Point – Naught

(c) Both (a) and (b) (d) None of these

35. What are the constituent elements of Simon's Flow Chart that are the components of Management System?

(a) Planning (b) Staffing

(c) Innovating (d) All of the Above

36. Which of the following are the characteristics of not for profit organizations according to Edward G. Evans?

(a) Financial sources derived from outside funding sources further than from sales of service.

(b) Funding preferences for collaborative projects.

(c) Organisations are public rather than private.

(d) All of the above

37. Which of the following are the criteria for defined open standard in W3C (2006)?

(a) Transparency and Impartiality

(b) Maintenance and Relevance

(c) Availability and Openness

(d) All of the above

38. Which of the following are pillars of Information literacy According to 'SCONUL' Seven pillars of Information Literacy?

(a) Gather (b) Identity

(c) Both (a) and (b) (d) None of these

39. Which of the following are the objectives of RRRLF?

(a) To promote library movement

(b) To promote reading habit

(c) Both (a) and (b)

(d) None of these

40. Identify the sequence of the 'Title' and 'Statement of Responsibility' are from the following :
    (a) Title Proper
    (b) Statement of Responsibility
    (c) General Material Designation
    (d) All of the above
41. In which year was the 'Third' edition of DDC Classification method published?
    (a) 1888 (b) 1890
    (c) 1882 (d) 1885
42. In which year was the '4th edition of DDC' classification method published?
    (a) 1889 (b) 1890
    (c) 1891 (d) 1895
43. In which year was the '5th edition of DDC' Classification method published?
    (a) 1892 (b) 1893
    (c) 1894 (d) 1895
44. What is the Main Class Number of "Philosophy" in "Nippon Decimal Classification" Scheme?
    (a) 100 (b) 200
    (c) 300 (d) 400
45. What is the main class number of "HISTORY" IN "Nippon Decimal Classification" Scheme?
    (a) 300 (b) 400
    (c) 200 (d) 600
46. Which country is the published of the "Nippon Decimal Classification" Scheme?
    (a) Russia (b) Africa
    (c) Japan (d) India

47. Who used the word "Bibliography" First?
    (a) C.A. Cutter
    (b) Lonis Jacob De Saint Charles
    (c) Henry La Fountain
    (d) S.R. Ranganathan
48. The term "Bibliography" was derived from ?
    (a) Greek word (b) French word
    (c) Roman word (d) Latin word
49. 'Telecommunication' is possible only though?
    (a) Wireless (b) Cables
    (c) Wires (d) All of the above
50. When was the era of Telecommunication without the wires started?
    (a) In 1905 (b) In 1910
    (c) In 1890 (d) In 1900
51. The term 'Library' is made of the word?
    (a) Liber (b) Libre
    (c) Libra (d) Libran
52. The word 'Libra' belongs to the language?
    (a) Latin (b) Roman
    (c) Russia (d) English
53. What is the meaning of the term 'Libra' in Hindi?
    (a) List of Book (b) Collection of Book
    (c) Stack of Book (d) House of Book
54. Who sponsors to 'BONET'?
    (a) National Informatic Centre
    (b) NISSAT
    (c) INSDOC
    (d) NASSDOC

55. 'Books in Print' is a national Database, which has been developed by :

(a) DELNET (b) UNESCO

(c) MEDLARS (d) RRRLF

56. What is the full name of 'CCF'?

(a) Common Computer Format

(b) Colon Classification Format

(c) Common Communication Format

(d) Common Cataloguing Format

57. What are various kinds of 'Subject Indexing Models":

(a) Authority Lists Based

(b) Keyword Based

(c) Both (a) and (b)

(d) None of these

58. When 'MARC-I' Format was commenced as a pilot project:

(a) 1966 (b) 1968

(c) 1957 (d) 1988

59. Which organization developed the 'MARC' format in 1966?

(a) National Library of UK

(b) American Library Association

(c) Library of Congress

(d) UNESCO

60. When AACR-I came out?

(a) 1966 (b) 1967

(c) 1968 (d) 1970

ANSWERS

1. (a)	2. (b)	3. (d)	4. (c)	5. (c)
6. (b)	7. (a)	8. (c)	9. (d)	10. (c)
11. (d)	12. (c)	13. (a)	14. (c)	15. (b)
16. (b)	17. (a)	18. (c)	19. (c)	20. (d)
21. (a)	22. (c)	23. (b)	24. (a)	25. (b)
26. (a)	27. (c)	28. (b)	29. (a)	30. (b)
31. (c)	32. (d)	33. (d)	34. (c)	35. (d)
36. (d)	37. (d)	38. (c)	39. (c)	40. (d)
41. (a)	42. (c)	43. (c)	44. (a)	45. (c)
46. (c)	47. (b)	48. (a)	49. (d)	50. (c)
51. (c)	52. (a)	53. (d)	54. (b)	55. (a)
56. (c)	57. (c)	58. (a)	59. (c)	60. (b)

Practice Set 4

1. What year was Dr. S. R. Ranganathan Born?
   (a) 12 August 1892 (b) 12 August 1890
   (c) 12 August 1882 (d) 12 August 1891
2. What was S. R. Ranganathan before becoming a Librarian?
   (a) A Philosopher (b) A Mathematician
   (c) A Scientist (d) A Researcher
3. The "Library for the People, of the People and by the People" is said about which types of libraries?
   (a) College Library (b) National Library
   (c) Public Library (d) Special Library
4. Under which Act, National Library of India receives books?
   (a) Delivery of Books Act, 1956
   (b) Delivery of Books Act, 1954
   (c) The Copyright Act, 1985
   (d) Registration of Books Act, 1887
5. Where is the National Library for Blind and Handicapped in India Located?
   (a) Dehradun (b) Kolkata
   (c) New Delhi (d) Chennai
6. Who is the Author of "Colon Classification" (CC) Scheme?
   (a) B.S. Kesavan (b) C.A. Cutter
   (c) Melvil Dewey (d) S.R. Ranganathan

7. In which year was the first edition of "Colon Classification" method published?
   (a) 1931 (b) 1933
   (c) 1934 (d) 1939
8. What year was "Raja Ram Mohan Ray Library Foundation" founded?
   (a) 1965 (b) 1976
   (c) 1972 (d) 1980
9. When 'Library Association in England' was set up?
   (a) 1880 (b) 1867
   (c) 1876 (d) 1877
10. When 'IASLIC' was setup in India?
   (a) 1955 (b) 1954
   (c) 1961 (d) 1952
11. Who was the Chairman of the Committee setup by IASLIC (1955)?
   (a) Dr. S.R. Ranganathan
   (b) Dr. S. L. Hora
   (c) B.S. Keswan
   (d) Radhakrishnan
12. 'PERRY' committee in Great Britain was setup for ?
   (a) Academic Libraries (b) Special Libraries
   (c) Industrial Libraries (d) National Libraries
13. Why 'Lal Committee' was mainly setup?
   (a) D. Lib. Science (b) B. Lib. Science
   (c) M. Lib. Science (d) Library Training
14. Who was the first chairman of UGC?
   (a) G. Bhattacharya (b) C.D. Deshmukh
   (c) S. R. Ranganathan (d) S. Radhakrishnan

15. When University Grant Commission (UGC) was setup?
    (a) 1953 (b) 1948
    (c) 1954 (d) 1961
16. Collection and provision of information from various sources over a period of time is known as ?
    (a) Short Range Reference Service
    (b) Long Range Reference Service
    (c) Current Awareness Service
    (d) Translation Service
17. The number of the States in India having Library Legislation?
    (a) 19 (b) 15
    (c) 18 (d) 22
18. In India public library developments as a movement was initially started from :
    (a) Madras (b) Culcutta
    (c) Baroda (d) Maharashtra
19. In India 'Book Week' is celebrated in the month of :
    (a) Janurary (b) March
    (c) April (d) November
20. Five laws of library science was first published in :
    (a) 1926 (b) 1928
    (c) 1931 (d) 1939
21. The arrangement of Main Entries in the classified catalogue is :
    (a) By a Classification Scheme
    (b) According to the Author
    (c) According to the Subject
    (d) None of these

22. The most important aspect of the management is :
    (a) Cost Benefit Analysis
    (b) Budget
    (c) Performance Analysis
    (d) All of the above
23. The grant from the UGC for the Academic Libraries is called :
    (a) Regular Grant (b) Ad-hoc Grant
    (c) Alan Grant (d) None of these
24. Thesis is an example of :
    (a) Micro Document (b) Conventional Document
    (c) Metadata (d) None of these
25. The Zero Based Budget was first prepared in :
    (a) 1980 (b) 1965
    (c) 1958 (d) 1970
26. A catalogue of Books Related to places is :
    (a) Corporate catalogue
    (b) Title catalogue
    (c) Topographical catalogue
    (d) Trade catalogue
27. A database is a collection of :
    (a) E-journals
    (b) Records in Machine Readable form
    (c) E-books
    (d) None of these
28. In a library scheme of collection, Number are devised and maintained by:
    (a) Technical Section (b) Reference Section
    (c) Circulation Section (d) Referral Section

29. How many part are there in 13 digits ISBN Number?
    (a) Seven (b) Nine
    (c) Eight (d) Five
30. Open Access System was first initiated by :
    (a) Lenine Libraries (b) British Library
    (c) Library of Congress (d) British Museum
31. Which of the following types memory is volatile?
    (a) RAM (b) ROM
    (c) CD-ROM (d) None of these
32. Canon of modulation falls under :
    (a) Common (b) Array
    (c) Chain (d) Notation
33. Name the two states in India, where public library act was passed in 1989 :
    (a) Bihar and Uttar Pradesh
    (b) Kerala and Haryana
    (c) Goa and Maharashtra
    (d) Goa and Haryana
34. Dickinson came to India in year :
    (a) 1905 (b) 1921
    (c) 1918 (d) 1915
35. India office library located in :
    (a) Indian National Library, Kolkata
    (b) British Library, London
    (c) Library of Congress, USA
    (d) Banaras Hindu University, U.P.
36. Library cess is as a source of finance for which types of library :
    (a) Public Library (b) Special Library
    (c) Academic Library (d) National Library

37. Who was the chairman of the working group on libraries (1964) set up by planning commission :
    (a) B.S. Kesavan (b) S.R. Ranganathan
    (c) V.K.R.V. Rao (d) None of these
38. Where was the first 'one year' PG diploma course in Library Science in India started?
    (a) Delhi University
    (b) Jawahar Lal Nehru Univeristy
    (c) Madras University
    (d) Chennai University
39. Delhi Public Library established in the year :
    (a) 1956 (b) 1955
    (c) 1951 (d) 1949
40. National Library of India Inaugurated on :
    (a) 2nd March, 1950 (b) 1st February, 1953
    (c) 26th May, 1948 (d) 28th August, 1951
41. BNB and INB are the examples of Bibliographies :
    (a) Local (b) National
    (c) Regional (d) Trade
42. "Subject Guide to Books in Print" selects its subject headings from :
    (a) Classified Catalogue Code
    (b) Library of Congress Subject Headings
    (c) Search List of Subject Headings
    (d) American Library Association List
43. Library Literature is a Subject :
    (a) Index (b) Classification
    (c) Chain (d) Abstract
44. In 'MARC-21' Subject Access field are :

(a) 2xx (b) 4xx
(c) 3xx (d) 6xx

45. A work which is treated as a subject by itself is :
(a) Analytical Subject (b) Quasi Subject
(c) Macro Subject (d) Micro Subject

46. "India : A Reference Annual" is an :
(a) Year Book (b) Hand Book
(c) Dictionary (d) Gazzatteer

47. The 'Publisher of India' who's who is :
(a) Ministry of Finance (b) INFA Publications
(c) Publication Bureau (d) None of these

48. British National Bibliography is cumulated monthly and .... :
(a) Weekly (b) Yearly
(c) Annually (d) Half yearly

49. Reference Catalogue of Current Literature was funded in 1874 by :
(a) A. Panizzi (b) C.A. Cutter
(c) H.P. Luhn (d) Joseph Whitaker

50. Encyclopedia are of two types i.e. :
(a) General and Special
(b) General and Private
(c) Private and Government
(d) Local and National

51. Whitaker's Cumulative book list is a publication of :
(a) London (b) Great Britain
(c) Chicago (d) America

52. Delhi Public Library is a Joint effort of :
(a) Government of India and ILA
(b) Government of India and ALA

(c) Government of India and UNESCO

(d) Government of India and Delhi State Government

53. Who called Ranganathan's era as "Age of Ranganathan"?

(a) A. Panizzi (b) Melvil Dewey

(c) C.A. Cutter (d) W.C.B. Sayers

54. When did Ranganathan Retired from the Madras University :

(a) 1948 (b) 1944

(c) 1946 (d) 1950

55. Which of the following Journal was edited by S.R. Ranganathan?

(a) Annal of Library Science

(b) Library Science with Slant to documentation

(c) Both (a) and (b)

(d) None of these

56. Teaching continuum spreads from :

(a) Training to Indoctrination

(b) Conditioning to Indoctrination

(c) Introduction to Indoctrination

(d) All of the above

57. Generally the synopsis of the research id compared with human body. Inspite of the differences existed in its different parts, it must have :

(a) Functional continuity

(b) Formulation

(c) Formation

(d) Uniformity

58. Signal Learning of Gagne's model is based on :

(a) Skinnerian Theory

(b) Social Transformation
(c) Pavlovian conditioning
(d) None of these

59. Education is a powerful instrument of :
(a) Personal Information
(b) Social Information
(c) Both (a) and (b)
(d) None of these

60. In Research thesis the Importance of introduction is :
(a) It imbibes the importance of problem in it
(b) It explain the objectives of the problem
(c) Both (a) and (b)
(d) None of these

ANSWERS

1. (a)	2. (b)	3. (c)	4. (b)	5. (a)
6. (d)	7. (b)	8. (c)	9. (d)	10. (a)
11. (b)	12. (a)	13. (c)	14. (b)	15. (a)
16. (b)	17. (a)	18. (c)	19. (d)	20. (c)
21. (a)	22. (d)	23. (b)	24. (b)	25. (d)
26. (c)	27. (b)	28. (a)	29. (d)	30. (d)
31. (a)	32. (c)	33. (b)	34. (d)	35. (b)
36. (a)	37. (c)	38. (c)	39. (c)	40. (b)
41. (b)	42. (c)	43. (a)	44. (d)	45. (b)
46. (a)	47. (b)	48. (c)	49. (d)	50. (a)
51. (b)	52. (c)	53. (d)	54. (b)	55. (c)
56. (b)	57. (a)	58. (c)	59. (c)	60. (c)

Practice Set 5

1. The 'Scientific Management' is centred on which of the following in an organization?
   (a) Production, Working efficiency and Stop loss
   (b) Motivation in the workers
   (c) Institutional structure
   (d) None of these
2. Who enunciated X and Y Theory of management?
   (a) Paul Outlet (b) L.P. Luhn
   (c) Peter Drucker (d) D. Mc. Gregor
3. Mc Gregor is concerned with which school of thoughts of management?
   (a) Quality management
   (b) Classical
   (c) Human relations
   (d) Scientific management
4. Henry Fayol is concerned with which school of thoughts of management?
   (a) Social system (b) Classical
   (c) System management(d) System analysis
5. Network system of circulation was started first in which country?
   (a) India (b) Canada
   (c) USA (d) Africa
6. What is the name of the software package developed by INFLIBNET?

(a) SOUL (b) Sanjay

(c) LibSys (d) E-granthalaya

7. What is the name of the software which is an Augmented version of CDS/ISIS?

(a) Librarian (b) SOUL

(c) Sanjay (d) None of these

8. What is the main components of Information Technology?

(a) Communication Technology

(b) Computer Technology

(c) Network Technology

(d) All of the above

9. When was the term information technology first enunciated?

(a) 1990 (b) 1975

(c) 1995 (d) 2005

10. What is the unit of the Rate of Communication data on the channel?

(a) bsp (b) bbs

(c) bps (d) Pdb

11. Which university changed the Diploma to Degree Course first in India in 1958?

(a) Aligarh Muslim University

(b) Banaras Hindu University

(c) University of Delhi

(d) Punjab University

12. What was the name of the father of Dr. S.R.Ranganathan?

(a) Sayali Ranganathan

(b) N. Ramamrit Ayyer

(c) Sayli Ramamrit Ranganathan Ayyer

(d) None of these

13. What was the name of the wife of Dr. S.R. Ranganathan?

(a) Kasturva (b) Nirmala

(c) Sapna (d) Sharda

14. In the name of Ranganathan the word Sayali Represents the name of his :

(a) Father (b) Mother

(c) Village (d) Town

15. "Library week in India" is organized every year during the period of :

(a) 14th November to 20th November

(b) 20th November to 25th November

(c) 21st November to 28th November

(d) 11th November to 19th November

16. Who was the teacher of Dr. S.R. Ranganathan in London?

(a) Anthony Pannizzi (b) W.C.B. Sayers

(c) Melvil Dewey (d) H.E. Bliss

17. Which university converted D. Lit on Dr. S.R. Ranganathan?

(a) London University

(b) Oxford University

(c) Banaras Hindu University

(d) Madras University

18. Which association was founded by Dr. S.R. Ranganathan?

(a) Indian Library Association

(b) American Library Association

(c) Calcutta Library Association

(d) Madras Library Association

19. Who is the first Emeritus Professor in Library and Information Science in India?

(a) P. N. Kaula (b) B.S. Kesvan

(c) S.R. Ranganathan (d) J.S. Sharma

20. Who is the co-worker of Dr. S. R. Ranganathan in the following :

(a) J.S. Sharma (b) P.N. Kaula

(c) M.A. Gopinath (d) None of these

21. Who are the main users of the University Libraries?

(a) Researcher (b) Student

(c) Faculty members (d) None of these

22. 'Book for All' is the same according to which law of library science?

(a) Books for Use

(b) Every book and its readers

(c) Books are for use

(d) Every book readers

23. The Five Law of Library Science by Ranganathan is an example of :

(a) Primary Research (b) Fundamental Research

(c) Analytical Research (d) Alphabetical Research

24. When 'Delivery of Books Act' was revised in India?

(a) 1961 (b) 1959

(c) 1956 (d) 1958

25. In which year W.Borden started a Refresher Course for libraries?

(a) 1916 (b) 1912

(c) 1911 (d) 1921

26. The word classification is derived from the Latin word?
(a) Classes (b) Classic
(c) Class (d) Clame

27. The real meaning of "Philosophical Scheme" is based on :
(a) Psychology
(b) Only Philosophy
(c) Philosophy and Logic
(d) None of these

28. The classification of the things according to size, colour etc. is called :
(a) Artificial Classification
(b) Natural Classification
(c) Historical Classification
(d) Logical Classification

29. Logical Classification means division on :
(a) Terminology and Logic Science
(b) Psychology and Terminology
(c) Logic and Psychology
(d) Philosophy and Logic

30. Who was the deviser of British Museum Code?
(a) AACR-2 Code (b) C.A. Cutter's Code
(c) A. Pannizzi Code (d) None of these

31. Who was the author of the code rules for a Dictionary Catalogue?
(a) H.E. Bliss (b) C.A. Cutter
(c) J.D. Browne (d) S.R. Ranganathan

32. The name of 'Miss Margaret Mnn' is mainly related with :
(a) Management (b) Software Developer

(c) Cataloguing (d) Classification

33. In which year the first edition of "American Library Association" (ALA) code was published?
(a) 1893 (b) 1890
(c) 1974 (d) 1899

34. When was International conference on cataloguing principles (ICCP) held ?
(a) 1961 (b) 1965
(c) 1957 (d) 1952

35. In which year the AACR was established?
(a) 1911 (b) 1901
(c) 1908 (d) 1913

36. In the main entry by "CCC", what is written in leading section?
(a) Accession Number (b) Call Number
(c) Book Number (d) Class Number

37. Class Index Entry entries are derived from :
(a) Class Number (b) Call Number
(c) Book Number (d) Accession Number

38. 'Information Retrieval' was first used in which year?
(a) 1948 (b) 1961
(c) 1955 (d) 1950

39. In which year the term "Information Science" was coined?
(a) 1965 (b) 1959
(c) 1957 (d) 1971

40. 'BNB' used which classification scheme?
(a) Universal Decimal Classification
(b) Colon Classification
(c) International Classification

(d) Dewey Decimal Classification

41. Who is the director of Public Libraries in India, according to the Library Legislation of India?

(a) The President of India

(b) The Prime Minister

(c) Chief Executive at State Level

(d) State Governor

42. Proper organization of reading material and efficient charging system is the implication of :

(a) Fourth Law of Library Science

(b) First Law of Library Science

(c) Second Law of Library Science

(d) Fifth Law of Library Science

43. According to Ranganathan the percentage of total money of the library budget to be spend on the reading materials should be :

(a) 20% (b) 40%

(c) 35% (d) 50%

44. The Patent are regarded as :

(a) Territory Sources (b) Secondary Sources

(c) Primary Sources (d) None of these

45. The frequency of "Indian National Bibliography" is :

(a) Annualy (b) Quarterly

(c) Weekly (d) Monthly

46. According to Colon Classification 'V' is known as :

(a) Religion (b) Philosophy

(c) History (d) Literature

47. According to Decimal Classification '200' is known as:

(a) Religion (b) Literature

(c) Drama (d) Fiction

48. The tracing section helps to identify the :
(a) Main entry (b) Added entry
(c) Class Index entry (d) General subject entry

49. "Shodhganga" is repository of :
(a) E-books (b) E-thesis
(c) E-communication (d) E-journals

50. Local point for 'DEVSIS' in the India as :
(a) DRDO
(b) NASSDOC
(c) National Information Centre (NIC)
(d) None of these

51. 'INIS' online services are available since ?
(a) 1980 (b) 1985
(c) 1960 (d) 1999

52. 'AGRIS' situated at :
(a) America (b) Somaliya
(c) Rome (d) New York

53. 'AGROVOC' was first appeared in :
(a) 1983 (b) 1990
(c) 1985 (d) 1977

54. Father of positivistic mode of thinking is :
(a) Kautilya
(b) August Comte
(c) Chandra Gupt Maurya
(d) None of these

55. Scientific method of research is a strong path, for reaching up to the door of :
(a) Truth (b) Analysis Concept
(c) Action (d) Re-action

56. Interview questioning is :
   (a) Written (b) Verbal
   (c) Print (d) None of these
57. 'Questionnaire' is a tool of :
   (a) Data Collection (b) Interview
   (c) Hypothesis (d) Observation
58. Main function of research design is :
   (a) Collection of Data
   (b) It is helpful
   (c) It provides blue print
   (d) None of these
59. "The Good Society" is written by :
   (a) Melvil Dewey (b) R. Bellah
   (c) Bliss (d) Cutter
60. Motivation Hygine Theory appeared in :
   (a) 1965 (b) 1960
   (c) 1968 (d) 1970

ANSWERS

1. (a)	2. (d)	3. (c)	4. (b)	5. (c)
6. (a)	7. (c)	8. (d)	9. (a)	10. (c)
11. (a)	12. (b)	13. (d)	14. (c)	15. (a)
16. (b)	17. (c)	18. (d)	19. (a)	20. (c)
21. (a)	22. (b)	23. (b)	24. (c)	25. (b)
26. (b)	27. (c)	28. (a)	29. (d)	30. (c)
31. (b)	32. (c)	33. (a)	34. (a)	35. (c)
36. (b)	37. (a)	38. (d)	39. (b)	40. (d)
41. (c)	42. (a)	43. (b)	44. (c)	45. (d)
46. (c)	47. (a)	48. (b)	49. (b)	50. (c)
51. (a)	52. (c)	53. (c)	54. (b)	55. (a)
56. (b)	57. (a)	58. (c)	59. (b)	60. (c)

Practice Set 6

1. Open Journal Access System in India is mainly managed by :
   (a) Information Library Network (INFLIBNET)
   (b) National Information Center (NIC)
   (c) Developing Library Network (DELNET)
   (d) Raja Ram Mohan Roy Library Foundation (RRRLF)
2. Catalogue is referred as a :
   (a) Method (b) Analytical
   (c) Tool (d) System
3. Which of the following is not a Computer Programming Language?
   (a) C (b) C+
   (c) C++ (d) ASCII
4. According to Colon Classification 'J' is known as :
   (a) Literature (b) Religion
   (c) Agricultural (d) History
5. Digital Library Functions incorporates :
   (a) Storage and management
   (b) Creating and capturing
   (c) Abstracting and reviewing
   (d) All of the above
6. Which of the following is not the stalwarts of Descriptive Theory?
   (a) Melvil Dewey (b) H.P. Luhn
   (c) Ranganathan (d) C.A. Cutter

7. Who devised one place theory?
   (a) Henry La Fontain (b) J.D. Browne
   (c) C.A. Cutter (d) Peter Drucker
8. Which one is the right combination?
   (a) CC is almost faceted
   (b) UDC is freely faceted
   (c) DDC is almost enumerative
   (d) None of these
9. On which the structure of main class in DDC is based?
   (a) Chart of Learning (b) List of Subject
   (c) List of Title (d) Classification Method
10. Which is the oldest classification scheme?
   (a) Expensive Classification
   (b) Subject Classification
   (c) Colon Classification
   (d) Dewey Decimal Classification
11. How many quadrants the spiral of scientific method has?
   (a) Seven (b) Five
   (c) Four (d) Three
12. Which is the digit of least ordinal value of CC :
   (a) Comma [,] (b) Equal sign [=]
   (c) Arrester [ )] (d) Starter [( ]
13. In which year the 'chain indexing' was announced?
   (a) 1936 (b) 1938
   (c) 1940 (d) 1941
14. When was 'DRTC' founded and with whose help?
   (a) 1962, Manalanobis (b) 1961, Govindana
   (c) 1957, Bhattacharya (d) 1955, Ranganathan

15. What is the sequential order of 'PMEST'?
    (a) Of modulation
    (b) Of increasing concreteness
    (c) Of decreasing concreteness
    (d) None of these
16. Indology is an example of :
    (a) Fusion (b) Cluster
    (c) Both (a) and (b) (d) None of these
17. A slanted abstract is :
    (a) One that is written for a specific kind of user
    (b) An abstract of a biased article
    (c) A critical event of an article
    (d) None of these
18. "Research method" an example of :
    (a) Selection (b) Fusion
    (c) Cluster (d) Distillation
19. The book AACR-2 has two parts namely:
    (a) Alphabetical and Classified
    (b) Description, Determination of Heading
    (c) Rule part, Description part
    (d) None of these
20. In AACR-2, the entry element for government is the :
    (a) Head of the government
    (b) Geographical are the country
    (c) Geographical was country
    (d) None of these
21. Indexing and Abstracting Services come under which services?
    (a) Reference Services (b) Translation
    (c) Documentation (d) Analysis

22. In chain procedure connecting symbol sign by which type links :
    (a) False Link (b) Sought Link
    (c) Unsought Link (d) Missing Link
23. 'PRECIS' has been originated from :
    (a) Uniterm Indexing (b) SLIC
    (c) Chain Index (d) Chain procedure
24. The Thesaurus for Index means :
    (a) List of concept (b) Dictionary of word
    (c) Subject Analysis (d) Controlled Vocabulary
25. Formation of subject headings is performed in PRECIS by :
    (a) Computer (b) Human Index
    (c) System Analysis (d) AACR-2
26. Who developed "Seven Facet of Information Literacy":
    (a) Christine Susan Bruce
    (b) MaC Fordown
    (c) C.A. Cutter
    (d) George R. Vilson
27. In which year the term 'Information Seeking' coined by T.D. Wilson?
    (a) 1979 (b) 1984
    (c) 1981 (d) 1890
28. "Indian Library Review" is a blog of :
    (a) Indian Library Association (ILA)
    (b) National Library of Indian, Kolkata
    (c) Madras Library Association
    (d) National Information System
29. In Colon Classification (6th Edition) the phase relation digit 'b' shows :

(a) Bias (b) General
(c) Array (d) Difference

30. Which is not the part of 'CPU' ?
(a) Mouse (b) Keyboard
(c) Printer (d) All of above

31. Information for all programme was launched by :
(a) MEDLARS (b) INIS
(c) UNESCO (d) ALA

32. AACR-2 is replaced by :
(a) British Library
(b) Library of Congress
(c) Resource Description and Access
(d) AACR-3

33. 'Europa World of Learning' is :
(a) Institutional Directory
(b) Telephone Directory
(c) Geographical Directory
(d) Historical Directory

34. D. Base is :
(a) Translation Software
(b) Application Software
(c) Digital Software
(d) System Software

35. Raja Ram Mohan Roy National Agency for 'ISBN' is located at :
(a) Kolkata (b) Chennai
(c) Delhi (d) Ahmadabad

36. 'Bern Convention' (1886) is concerned with :
(a) Trade (b) Standard
(c) Copyright (d) None of these

37. The Database Indian patents is published by :
(a) NISCAIR (b) NASSDOC
(c) MEDLARS (d) UNESCO

38. Which one of the following is not tool for "Book Selection"?
(a) British Books in print
(b) Publishers weekly
(c) Data India
(d) None of these

39. 'National Book Trust' is an autonomous organization functioning now under the aegis of :
(a) Ministry of Education
(b) Ministry of HRD
(c) Ministry of Cultural
(d) Ministry of Art

40. Linux is an example of :
(a) Database software
(b) Translation software
(c) Application software
(d) System software

41. Identify the author of "Essays of an Information Scientist" from among the following:
(a) C.A. Cutter (b) F.W. Lancaster
(c) George R. Tarry (d) Eugene Garfield

42. Dance's Helical Spiral Communication model is a :
(a) None-Linear (b) Classical
(c) Linear (d) Dimensional

43. Who has coined the term 'Information Society' from the following :
(a) Lancaster (b) Macforlan
(c) Fritz Machlup (d) B.C. Vickery

44. Maulana Abul Kalam Azad the then Union Education Minister formally declared on of the following libraries open to the public on 2nd February 1953 :

    (a) National Library of India, Kolkata
    (b) National Information Centre, Delhi
    (c) National Documentation Centre
    (d) Khuda Baksh Public Library, Patna

45. The concept of select Dissemination of Information (SDI) was enunciated by :

    (a) Melvil Dewey (b) H.P. Luhn
    (c) S.R. Ranganathan (d) C.A. Cutter

46. Current Awareness Bulletin is :

    (a) Primary Source Bulletin
    (b) Secondary Source Bulletin
    (c) Trend Report
    (d) Annually Bulletin

47. In 1966, The MARC as a Pilot Project was launched by:

    (a) Library of Congress
    (b) Indian Library Association
    (c) American Library Association
    (d) The British Museum Library

48. 'SAARC' documentation centre was established in :

    (a) 1972 (b) 1999
    (c) 1985 (d) 1994

49. Ranganathan's Cannon of Classification as grouped into three planes of work are :

    (a) Idea, Verbal and National
    (b) Verbal, Idea and National
    (c) National, Idea and Verbal
    (d) None of these

50. The first block in 'ISBN' is a :
(a) Title Identifier
(b) Subject Identifier
(c) Geographical Identifier
(d) Biographical Identifier

51. The method of Reducing the Physical size of a block of Information is called :
(a) Data compression (b) Data Analysis
(c) Data Analytical (d) Data Communication

52. Which one of the following is a volatile memory:
(a) ROM (b) RAM
(c) SOM (d) CD-ROM

53. 'LYCOS' is a :
(a) Search Machine (b) Search App
(c) Search Engine (d) Database

54. The ability to travel between electronic documents using any number of alternative paths to find relevant information is known as :
(a) Metadata (b) Searching
(c) Linking (d) Browsing

55. A questionnaire designed with open-ended questions is known as :
(a) Flexible (b) Structure
(c) Structured (d) Unstructured

56. None Sampling Error (NSE) are referred to as errors :
(a) Qualification (b) Management
(c) Quality (d) Quantification

57. Intellectual Property Rights (IPR) cover :
(a) Patents (b) Copyright
(c) Both (a) and (b) (d) None of these

58. The libraries identified by "INFLIBNET' to Act as a Document Delivery Centre are :
    (a) University of Hyderabad, Hyderabad
    (b) Punjab University, Chandigarh
    (c) Both (a) and (b)
    (d) None of these
59. Which of the following are Trade Bibliographies?
    (a) Books in Print (b) Indian Books in Prints
    (c) Both (a) and (b) (d) None of these
60. Which of the following are maintained to provide select dissemination of information (SDI) Service?
    (a) Document Profile (b) User Profile
    (c) Both (a) and (b) (d) None of these

ANSWERS

1. (a)	2. (c)	3. (d)	4. (c)	5. (d)
6. (c)	7. (b)	8. (c)	9. (a)	10. (d)
11. (c)	12. (c)	13. (b)	14. (a)	15. (c)
16. (b)	17. (a)	18. (d)	19. (b)	20. (b)
21. (c)	22. (a)	23. (b)	24. (d)	25. (a)
26. (a)	27. (c)	28. (b)	29. (a)	30. (d)
31. (c)	32. (c)	33. (a)	34. (b)	35. (c)
36. (c)	37. (a)	38. (c)	39. (b)	40. (d)
41. (d)	42. (a)	43. (c)	44. (a)	45. (b)
46. (c)	47. (a)	48. (d)	49. (a)	50. (c)
51. (a)	52. (b)	53. (c)	54. (b)	55. (d)
56. (d)	57. (c)	58. (c)	59. (c)	60. (c)

Practice Set 7

1. The following are used as Transmission media for voice/data communication :
   (a) Optic wire (b) Copper wide
   (c) Co-axial cables (d) All of the above
2. The components in delegation as authority are :
   (a) Authority (b) Responsibility
   (c) Accountability (d) All of the above
3. Which of the following are modes of formation of subjects?
   (a) Agglomeration (b) Denutation
   (c) Both (a) and (b) (d) None of the above
4. Who wrote the foreword to the first edition of "Five Laws of Library Science"?
   (a) P.S. Sivaswamy Ayyer
   (b) C.A. Cutter
   (c) B.S. Kesavan
   (d) G Bhattacharya
5. "Keesings Record of World Events" is published from:
   (a) New York (b) London
   (c) Washington D.C. (d) India
6. The 'Letter by Letter' method of alphabetization in dictionary catalogue is known as :
   (a) Nothing before something
   (b) Something before nothing
   (c) Something after more
   (d) All of the above

7. Identify the symbol of "Spiritual Experience and Mysticism" as given by CC :

(a) Δ (b) <

(c) ((d))

8. Which of the following is indicated in the 3rd digit of DDC 3rd summary?

(a) Index (b) Section

(c) Notation (d) Division

9. Which of the following are the non-parametric tests?

(a) Spearman correlation coefficient

(b) Chi-square test

(c) Both (a) and (b)

(d) None of these

10. Transborde data flow includes movements across national boundaries :

(a) Machine readable data for processing storage or retrieval

(b) Machine readable data or magnetic tapes

(c) Machine readable data on discs

(d) All the above

11. Which of the following are the cannon for characteristics as enunciated by S.R. Ranganathan?

(a) Canon of relevance

(b) Canon of perinanance

(c) Canon of differentiation

(d) All of the above

12. Arrange the following libraries in the chronological sequence of their emergence:

(a) Rampur Raza Library, Uttar Pradesh

(b) Asiatic Society Library, Bombay

(c) Connemora Public Library, Chennai
(d) All of the above

13. Why the investigators tend to carryout searches themselves?
(a) They are unwarde of information sources
(b) They have time to assess and digest individual papers
(c) Both (a) and (b)
(d) None of these

14. 'Dulphy method' is used for :
(a) Analysis (b) Forecasting
(c) Evaluation (d) Finance

15. Staff formula for university and college in India have been developed by :
(a) H.P. Luhn (b) B.S. Kesavan
(c) M.A. Gopinathan (d) S.R. Ranganathan

16. Motivation and fatique studies under :
(a) Scientific school of thought
(b) Numan resource school thought
(c) Human relation school thought
(d) All of the above

17. The five element of 'marketing mix' are product, place, price, promotion and :
(a) Researcher (b) Staff
(c) User (d) Finance

18. 'TQM' stands for :
(a) Total questions management
(b) Total query manage
(c) Total Quality Management
(d) None of these

19. 'MIS' stands for :
    (a) Management Information Symbol
    (b) Manage Informatic System
    (c) Management Inform System
    (d) Management Information System

20. The concept of "Quality Circle" was developed in :
    (a) America (b) China
    (c) Japan (d) India

21. 'Dublin Core' metadata consists of :
    (a) 15 elements (b) 11 elements
    (c) 21 elements (d) 10 elements

22. Which of the following is not a section of a main entry in 'CCC' (5th edition)?
    (a) Area Section (b) Note Section
    (c) Name Section (d) Tracing Section

23. E-shodh sindhu is a :
    (a) Library Application Software
    (b) Ganga River
    (c) A consortium
    (d) Internet Service

24. National Register of Translators is maintained by :
    (a) National Translation Mission
    (b) DRDO
    (c) Central Translation Bureau
    (d) Raja Ram Mohan Ray Translation Centre

25. 'Contents by Journals' is an example of :
    (a) Translation Services (TS)
    (b) Select Dissemination Information (SDI)
    (c) Current Awareness Service (CAS)
    (d) Document Delivery Service (DDS)

26. Which of the following is a publication of Central Reference Library, Kolkata?
    (a) Library Tools (b) Index - Indiana
    (c) Library Index (d) Index - Indian
27. Critical - Incident Technique primarily concentrates on :
    (a) Content Analysis
    (b) Job Analysis
    (c) A Small Number of Individuals
    (d) System Analysis
28. The Book "The Measurement and Evaluation of Library Science" is written by :
    (a) C.A. Cutter and W. Wilson
    (b) H.P. Luhn and F.W. Lancaster
    (c) S.L. Baker and F.W. Lancaster
    (d) None of these
29. 'African Recorder' is which type of publication?
    (a) News Digest
    (b) Law Digest
    (c) Bibliographical Digest
    (d) Computer Directory
30. 'Three Card System' was developed by :
    (a) J.D. Browne (b) C.A. Cutter
    (c) Melvil Dewey (d) S.R. Ranganathan
31. "Disaster Recovery" is a Negative driving factor for introducing good record management in organizations. The above statement is true or falls?
    (a) True (b) False
    (c) Both (a) and (b) (d) None of these
32. Ownership of property depends on :

(a) Contracts paper (b) Written Title Deeds
(c) Verbal Title Deeds (d) None of these

33. Which of the following statement is incorrect?
    (a) Liability is a driving force towards the need for good record management
    (b) Contacts are valuable assets that need to be managed
    (c) Protection against litigation is not important
    (d) None of these

34. The following are used as tools for vocabulary control in indexing:
    (a) List of subject headings
    (b) Thesaurus
    (c) Both (a) and (b)
    (d) None of these

35. The following states in India do not have library legislation:
    (a) Assam (b) Bihar
    (c) Uttar Pradesh (d) Goa

36. The national level association for special libraries are :
    (a) ASLIB (b) IASLIC
    (c) Both (a) and (b) (d) None of these

37. Which of the following are library network?
    (a) DELNET (b) OCLC
    (c) DRDO (d) Both (a) and (b)

38. The Theories Relating to motivation are :
    (a) Maslow Theory
    (b) McGregor Theory 'X' and Theory 'Y'
    (c) Both (a) and (b)
    (d) None of these

39. A library which is considered as the National library of the United States is :
    (a) Located at Washington D C
    (b) Library of Congress
    (c) The British Library
    (d) Both (a) and (b)
40. The Research Process are :
    (a) Hypothesis, Theory, Law and Axion
    (b) Theory, Hypothesis, Law and Axion
    (c) Hypothesis, Law, Theory and Axion
    (d) None of these
41. Who is sponsor of 'NASSDOC'?
    (a) UNESCO (b) CSIR
    (c) ICSSR (d) RRRLF
42. When did 'SENDOC' established?
    (a) 1976 (b) 1971
    (c) 1975 (d) 1981
43. Where is 'SENDOC' situated?
    (a) Calcutta (b) Mumbai
    (c) Ahmadabad (d) Hyderabad
44. 'INSDOC' stands for:
    (a) Indian National Scientific Documentation Centre
    (b) Indian National Science Documentation Centre
    (c) Indian national Scientist Document Centre
    (d) None of these
45. 'SDI' is a kind of which service?
    (a) Internet Service
    (b) Data Collection
    (c) Translation Service
    (d) Current Awareness Service

46. What is the Role of Information Centre :
    (a) Collect and Disseminate the Information
    (b) Collect the Information
    (c) Storage of the Information
    (d) None of these
47. 'INSDOC' was fist established under the administration of :
    (a) Indian Abstract Centre
    (b) Indian Institute of Science
    (c) National Physical Laboratory
    (d) National informatics Centre
48. Patent Information System (PIS), Nagpur is :
    (a) Material Oriented (b) Number Oriented
    (c) Subject Oriented (d) Mission Oriented
49. Where is Science Information Centre of UGC located?
    (a) RRRLF (b) NASSDOC
    (c) INSDOC (d) DRDO
50. In which year 'DRTC' was established?
    (a) 1976 (b) 1971
    (c) 1951 (d) 1962
51. Where are 'DRTC' established?
    (a) Bangalore (b) Chennai
    (c) New Delhi (d) Kolkata
52. What is the main aim of 'DRTC' in India?
    (a) Research and Training Programme in Classification
    (b) Research and Training Programme in Documentation
    (c) Research and Training Programme in Catalogue
    (d) None of these

53. 'UBC' stands for :
    (a) Universal Bibliographical Control
    (b) Universal Biographical Control
    (c) Universal Book Centre
    (d) None of these
54. What is 'UNISIST'?
    (a) Indian information Centre
    (b) World Information Centre
    (c) Indian Indexing Programme
    (d) International information System on Science and Technology
55. Who was first director of DRTC in 1962?
    (a) G. Bhattacharya (b) S.R. Ranganathan
    (c) B.S. Kesavan (d) T. Vishwanathan
56. Which one is the International Information System in Nuclear Science?
    (a) UNESCO (b) DRDO
    (c) ISRO (d) INIS
57. Which organization co-operates the INIS programme?
    (a) IFLA (b) IAEA
    (c) UNESCO (d) MEDLARS
58. 'NICNET' is a programme of :
    (a) India (b) Japan
    (c) USA (d) Canada
59. Where is the Centre of 'NICMAP'?
    (a) New Delhi (b) Calcutta
    (c) Mumbai (d) Banglore
60. How Research is started?
    (a) From a question or a problem of some short
    (b) From a design

(c) From a hypothesis

(d) From a observation

ANSWERS

1. (d)	2. (d)	3. (c)	4. (a)	5 (b)
6. (d)	7. (a)	8. (b)	9. (c)	10. (d)
11. (d)	12. (d)	13. (b)	14. (b)	15. (d)
16. (a)	17. (b)	18. (c)	19. (d)	20. (c)
21. (a)	22. (c)	23. (c)	24. (a)	25. (c)
26. (b)	27. (c)	28. (c)	29. (a)	30. (d)
31. (a)	32. (b)	33. (a)	34. (c)	35. (a)
36. (c)	37. (d)	38. (c)	39. (d)	40. (a)
41. (c)	42. (b)	43. (d)	44. (a)	45. (d)
46. (a)	47. (c)	48. (a)	49. (c)	50. (d)
51. (a)	52. (b)	53. (a)	54. (d)	55. (b)
56. (d)	57. (b)	58. (a)	59. (d)	60. (a)

Practice Set 8

1. High level language refers to :
   (a) Programming language
   (b) High level language
   (c) Low level language
   (d) Machine language
2. What is 'FORTRAN' stands for :
   (a) For Train (b) Formula Transmission
   (c) Formula Translation (d) None of these
3. What is Bug?
   (a) Computer virus
   (b) None compactibility between software and hardware
   (c) Search engine
   (d) None of these
4. Micro CDS/ISIS is a :
   (a) Information Package
   (b) Communication Package
   (c) Command Package
   (d) Menu-driven Package
5. Which honour was awarded to Dr. S.R. Ranganathan for his contributions in Library Software?
   (a) Padam Shri (b) Padam Bhushan
   (c) Novel (d) Gyan Peeth Puraskar
6. According to Ranganathan what should be the percentage of per capita teachers :

(a) 150% (b) 100%
(c) 300% (d) 200%

7. Who propounded classical theory of management?
(a) S.R. Ranganathan (b) Henry La Fountain
(c) C.A.Cutter (d) F.W. Taylor

8. Who is known as Dewey of Japan ?
(a) Ohio (b) Fujio
(c) Nagasaki (d) Hirosima

9. What is library of congress?
(a) National Public Library, USA
(b) National Library of USA
(c) The Central Library of USA
(d) National Library of UK

10. Which organization is the corporate author of 'UDC'?
(a) ALA (b) IFLA
(c) INIS (d) FID

11. Which is the Real Process to again knowledge from Information?
(a) Data, Information, Knowledge
(b) Information, Data, Knowledge
(c) Knowledge, Data, Information
(d) Data, Knowledge, Information

12. Who is the publisher of "Defense Science Journal"?
(a) SENDOC (b) DESIDOC
(c) NASSDOC (d) DRDO

13. Who devised the spiral of scientific method?
(a) C.A. Cutter (b) S.R. Ranganathan
(c) Melvil Dewey (d) B.S. Kesavan

14. Which type of research is begin done now days?

(a) Fundamental Research
(b) Basic Research
(c) Application Research
(d) Applied Research

15. Melvil Dewey related to which country?
(a) Britain (b) America
(c) Canada (d) Russia

16. In which year 'ASLIB' was founded in Britain?
(a) 1924 (b) 1928
(c) 1933 (d) 1939

17. In which year 'ILA' (Indian Library Association) was established?
(a) 1948 (b) 1921
(c) 1933 (d) 1935

18. Sadler Commission in India was setup in which year?
(a) 1918 (b) 1917
(c) 1914 (d) 1911

19. Who developed the 'Chain Procedure'?
(a) Peter Drucker (b) Melvil Dewey
(c) S.R. Ranganathan (d) George R. Tarry

20. What is the term from which the term documentation was changed round about 1930?
(a) Bibliography
(b) Information Service
(c) Documentation Service
(d) Reference Service

21. Break-down in verbal communication is described as:
(a) Contradiction (b) Entropy
(c) Short Circuit (d) None of these

22. The telephone model of communication was first developed in the area of :
    (a) Information Theory
    (b) Communication Theory
    (c) Classification Theory
    (d) Classified Theory

23. The 'Dada Saheb Phalke' Award for 2013 has been conferred on :
    (a) Amir Khan (b) Amitabh Bachchan
    (c) Gulzar (d) Lata Mangeshkar

24. The Acronym 'FTP' stands for :
    (a) File Transfer Procedure
    (b) File Transfer Protocol
    (c) File Tracking Protocol
    (d) None of these

25. Which one of the following is not a/an image file format?
    (a) GIE (b) CRE
    (c) GUI (d) EGP

26. The first web browser is :
    (a) World Wide Web (b) Search Engine
    (c) Internet Explorer (d) Firefox

27. When a computer is booting, 'BIOS' is loads to the memory by :
    (a) TCP/IP (b) CD-ROM
    (c) RAM (d) ROM

28. Which of the following is not the same as the other three?
    (a) Physical Address (b) Hardware Address
    (c) Mail Address (d) IP Address

29. Which of the following cities has been worst affected by Urban Smog in recent times?
(a) New York (b) Delhi
(c) Beising (d) Washington D C

30. The primary source of organic pollution in fresh water bodies is :
(a) Sewage effluents (b) Run-off urban area
(c) Both (a) and (b) (d) None of these

31. The National Disaster Management Authority functions under the Union Ministry of:
(a) Home Affairs
(b) Water Resource Ministry
(c) Environment Department
(d) Defense Ministry

32. Who among the following is the de facto executive head of the planning commission?
(a) Ministry of Planning Commission
(b) Chairman
(c) Deputy Chairman
(d) None of these

33. Education as a subject of legislation figures in the :
(a) State List (b) Catalogue List
(c) Union List (d) Concurrent List

34. Which of the following Universities has adopted the meta university concept?
(a) Delhi University
(b) Punjab University
(c) Banaras Hindu University
(d) Aligarh Muslim University

35. Which one of the following is considered a sign of motivated teaching?

(a) Student taking notes (b) Student asking questions
(c) Both (a) and (b) (d) None of these

36. Which one of the following is the best method of teaching?
(a) Demonstration (b) Lecture
(c) Discussion (d) None of these

37. Dyslexia is associated with :
(a) Behavioural disorder
(b) Reading disorder
(c) Mental disorder
(d) None of the above

38. Classroom communication is normally considered as:
(a) Effective (b) Affective
(c) Selective (d) Observative

39. Who among the following propounded the concept of paradigm?
(a) Von Thunen (b) Thomas Kuhn
(c) George R. Tarry (d) H.P. Luhn

40. In a thesis, figures and tables are included in :
(a) The text itself
(b) The appendix
(c) The concluding chapter
(d) None of these

41. Which of the following Journals was edited by S.R. Ranganathan?
(a) Annual of Library Science
(b) Library Science with Slant to documentation
(c) ABGILA
(d) All of the above

42. In which round the space category occurs?
(a) First (b) Last
(c) Middle (d) None of these

43. Who was the scientist who invited him to establish 'DRTC'?
(a) P.C. Mahalanobis (b) S.R. Ranganathan
(c) Peter Drucker (d) B.S. Kesavan

44. Which was the country where Ranganathan visited in 1948?
(a) USA (b) U.K.
(c) Japan (d) Russia

45. The first library periodicals in India is :
(a) Library Classification in India
(b) Library Journal in Library Science
(c) Library Miscellany (Quarterly) 1910-1913
(d) None of these

46. The 'Periodicity of Book Review Digest' is :
(a) Monthly (b) Yearly
(c) Annually (d) Weekly

47. "Library Quarterly" is a publication of :
(a) University of Calcutta
(b) University of Chicago
(c) Banaras Hindu University
(d) University of New York

48. Who first time used phrase "Reference Interview" :
(a) Paul Outlet (b) C.A. Cutter
(c) Margret Hultchins (d) None of these

49. Xerography was invented by :
(a) Henry La Fountain (b) Paul Outlet
(c) George R. Tarry (d) Chester F. Carlson

50. In DDC, The facet Indicators which combine facts are:
    (a) One basic subject and two isolate idea
    (b) Two or more basic or compound subjects
    (c) Both (a) and (b)
    (d) None of these
51. Which kind of the notation are used in DDC?
    (a) Pure (b) Mixed
    (c) General (d) All of the above
52. Relation between the Basic Subject is known as :
    (a) Common Isolate (b) Phase Relation
    (c) Intra Facet (d) Intra Array
53. Which kind of 'Notation' are used in 'CC'?
    (a) General (b) Pure
    (c) Mixed (d) None of these
54. The International Standard ISO-2709 is derived from :
    (a) MARC-1 (b) MRC-21
    (c) CCF (d) ANSI
55. A 'MAN' has :
    (a) One or two cables (b) Two Cables
    (c) Three Cables (d) Five Cables
56. The first commercial virus was :
    (a) E-scan (b) Brain
    (c) Quick Heal (d) Yankee Doodle
57. Password Security involves :
    (a) Identification (b) Authentication
    (c) Authorisation (d) All of the above
58. Which of the following has founded ERNET?
    (a) UNDP (b) MEDLARS
    (c) UNESCO (d) DRDO

59. The term 'Librametric' was proposed in :
    (a) 1958 (b) 1932
    (c) 1936 (d) 1948

60. Scalogram Analysis' was proposed in :
    (a) 1936 (b) 1952
    (c) 1948 (d) 1944

ANSWERS

1. (a)	2. (c)	3. (b)	4. (d)	5. (a)
6. (c)	7. (d)	8. (b)	9. (b)	10. (d)
11. (a)	12. (b)	13. (b)	14. (d)	15. (b)
16. (a)	17. (c)	18. (b)	19. (c)	20. (a)
21. (c)	22. (a)	23. (c)	24. (b)	25. (c)
26. (a)	27. (d)	28. (d)	29. (c)	30. (a)
31. (a)	32. (c)	33. (d)	34. (a)	35. (b)
36. (a)	37. (b)	38. (b)	39. (b)	40. (a)
41. (d)	42. (b)	43. (a)	44. (b)	45. (c)
46. (a)	47. (b)	48. (c)	49. (d)	50. (b)
51. (a)	52. (b)	53. (c)	54. (d)	55. (a)
56. (b)	57. (d)	58. (a)	59. (d)	60. (d)

Practice Set 9

1. The concept of Facet Analysis and Fundamental Categories deals with :
   (a) Laws (b) Principles
   (c) Device (d) None of these
2. In DDC, when not instructed in Schedule, –089 is used for Table :
   (a) Fifth (b) Four
   (c) Three (d) Two
3. What is "Law of Local Variation" Formulated by Dr. S.R. Ranganathan?
   (a) Five Laws (b) Phase Relation
   (c) Common Isolates (d) Basic Law
4. 'UNITERM' Index was given by :
   (a) M. Taube (b) S.R. Ranganathan
   (c) Henry La Fountain (d) Paul Outlet
5. The term 'Lexicography' is associated with :
   (a) Compilation of Encyclopedia
   (b) Compilation of Dictionaries
   (c) Compilation of handbook
   (d) Compilation of yearbook
6. "Psychology for Teacher" is a which kind of relation?
   (a) Common Isolates (b) Difference
   (c) Bias (d) Influence
7. In CC, the principle that help in the identification of personality category of :

(a) Neti-Neti Principles (b) Later in the Principles
(c) Cow-Calf Principles (d) None of these

8. According to S.R. Ranganathan, which category is the central core of a subject?
(a) Energy (b) Space
(c) Matter (d) Personality

9. In Madras University the first one year post graduate diploma course in Library Science in India started in year :
(a) 1939 (b) 1937
(c) 1931 (d) 1942

10. The Hierarchy Theory of motivation was conceived by :
(a) H.P. Luhn (b) Wan Evan
(c) Abraham Moslow (d) Peter Drucket

11. Delhi Public Library Was established in 1950 by :
(a) Delhi State Government
(b) Government of India and UNESCO Jointly
(c) Only Central Government of India
(d) None of these

12. Melvil Dewey first worked as a Library Assistant, When was student in which collage?
(a) Amherst College (b) Chicago College
(c) New York College (d) California College

13. The fundamental equation of Information Science has been put forward by :
(a) S.R. Ranganathan (b) Henry La fountain
(c) Robert Brooks (d) Melvil Dewey

14. Source, Massage, Transmitter and Receiver are the components of communication model developed by :

(a) George R. Tarry (b) Macswell
(c) Shannon Weaver (d) H.P. Luhn

15. Census Atlas National volume is an example of Atlas:
(a) National (b) International
(c) Local (d) Demographic

16. Routing of Periodicals is :
(a) Current Awareness Service
(b) Select Dissemination Information
(c) Translation Service
(d) Reference Service

17. The subject "Research Methodology" has been formed by which of the following modes?
(a) Loose Assemblage (b) Fusion
(c) Distillation (d) None of these

18. Boolean Logic was propounded by :
(a) H.P. Luhn (b) George Boole
(c) Henry La Fountain (d) C.A. Cutter

19. "IMCE" stands for :
(a) International Meeting Catalogue Express
(b) Indian Machine Catalogue Experts
(c) International Meeting of Cataloguing Experts
(d) International Metadata of Catalogue Experts

20. An Indispensable Function of Thesaurus is :
(a) Information Representation
(b) Representation of Relationship between concepts
(c) Data Representation
(d) Knowledge Representation

21. The library budget prepared without considering the previous years budget is :

(a) Line item budget (b) Performance budget

(c) Zero base budget (d) None of these

22. Data about data is known as :

(a) Analysis (b) Metadata

(c) Micro data (d) Analytical

23. The concept of micro photography was developed by:

(a) Benjimen Dancer (b) John Gutenberg

(c) Peter Drucker (d) Lancaster

24. Which among the following is a digital library software used in the creation of an Inhouse Digital Library?

(a) E-granthalaya (b) Sanjay

(c) Green Stone (d) Libsys

25. 'SSDC' referred to the National Documentation Centre now known as :

(a) SENDOC (b) NASSDOC

(c) DRDO (d) MEDLARS

26. Annual convention of 'INFLIBNET' organized to discuss the progress of Library Automation and Library Services is known as :

(a) BONET (b) CALIBER

(c) ISCON (d) RRRLF

27. Formulation of Research Hypothesis implies :

(a) Enumeration of postulates

(b) Enumeration of canon

(c) Formation of Tentative Generation

(d) None of these

28. 'Harzberg' is two factor theory deals with :

(a) Motivation

(b) Management

(c) Classification Theory

(d) Cataloguing Theory

29. Raja Ram Mohan Ray Library Foundation :
    (a) Promotes Public Library
    (b) Located at Kolkata
    (c) Both (a) and (b)
    (d) None of these
30. The "Principle of Literary Warrant" was propounded by :
    (a) M. Luther (b) M. Tuabe
    (c) W. Hulme (d) S.R. Ranganathan
31. Pre-natal catalogue means :
    (a) Simplified catalogue
    (b) Pre-publication classification list
    (c) Selective Cataloguing
    (d) Pre-publication cataloguing
32. The author who defined reference service as the process of establishing contact between a reader and his documents in a personal way is :
    (a) M. Tube (b) W.A. Katz
    (c) Melvil Dewey (d) B.S. Kesavan
33. Identify the odd one :
    (a) Index medicus (b) WWW
    (c) World of Learning (d) None of these
34. Which of the following is not correctly matched?
    (a) DELNET
    (b) Thesaurus
    (c) Digital Library - Print Material
    (d) ISBD
35. An entry is an Abstracting Journal consists of :
    (a) Analytical Citation
    (b) Bibliographic Citation

(c) Biographical Citation
(d) An Abstract and Bibliographic Citation

36. Technological gatekeeper is :
(a) An Informal Channel
(b) A Term Coined by T.J.
(c) Both (a) and (b)
(d) None of these

37. The National Library for the visually handicapped is located at :
(a) Dehradun (b) New Delhi
(c) Bangalore (d) Chennai

38. In which of following Network Topologies, all the computers are connected to a central computer :
(a) Bus (b) Ring
(c) Star (d) Peer to Peer

39. If the size of the study population is very small, the following sampling method will give better results :
(a) Random (b) Purposive
(c) Canon (d) Staffing

40. Formatting a document in computer means :
(a) Changing the font size only
(b) Adding new content
(c) Editing the content
(d) None of these

41. When was the Public Library Act passed in Goa?
(a) 1993 (b) 1989
(c) 1981 (d) 1981

42. When was the Public Library Act passed in Gujarat?
(a) 2005 (b) 2001
(c) 2010 (d) 1999

43. When was the Public Library Act passed in Mizoram?
    (a) 1989 (b) 1998
    (c) 2002 (d) 1993

44. When was the Public Library Act passed in Uttarakhand?
    (a) 2010 (b) 2008
    (c) 2005 (d) 1998

45. When was the Public Library Act passed in Kerala?
    (a) 1989 (b) 1991
    (c) 1985 (d) 1971

46. Which of the following factors does not impact teaching?
    (a) Socio-economic background of teachers and students
    (b) Teacher's information
    (c) Teacher's communication
    (d) Teacher's knowledge

47. Which of the following statements about teaching aids are correct?
    (a) They make teaching learning process interesting
    (b) They help in retaining concepts for longer duration
    (c) They help students learn better
    (d) All of these

48. Techniques used by a teacher to teach include:
    (a) Group work (b) Lecture
    (c) Self study (d) None of these

49. Achievement test are commonly used for the purpose of :
    (a) Making selections for a specific job
    (b) Assessing the amount of learning after teaching

(c) Both (a) and (b)
(d) None of these

50. A good teacher is one who :
(a) Give useful communication
(b) Gives useful information
(c) Inspires students to learn
(d) None of these

51. "Male and Female students perform equally well in a Numerical Aptitude Test". This statement indicates a:
(a) Null Hypothesis
(b) Observation Hypothesis
(c) Research Hypothesis
(d) None of these

52. The conclusions of which type of research cannot be generalized to other situations?
(a) Basic Research (b) Primary Research
(c) Historical Research (d) Experimental Research

53. Which of the following steps are required to design a questionnaire?
(a) Prepare a draft of Questionnaire
(b) Revision of the draft
(c) Writing primary and secondary aims of the study
(d) All of the above

54. Our knowledge is a collection of :
(a) A few stories that survive
(b) Some stories that we remember
(c) Both (a) and (b)
(d) None of these

55. Story telling is :

(a) A science
(b) In our gens
(c) The essence of what makes us human
(d) None of these

56. How the future will turn out to be depends upon the stories?
(a) Which are repeatedly narrated
(b) We collectively choose to believe in
(c) Both (a) and (b)
(d) None of these

57. Rational optimists :
(a) Are selfishly driven
(b) Are sensible and cheerful
(c) Look for opportunities
(d) All of the above

58. Humans become less selfish when :
(a) They work in solitude
(b) They work in large groups
(c) Both (a) and (b)
(d) None of these

ANSWERS

1. (b)	2. (a)	3. (d)	4. (a)	5. (b)
6. (c)	7. (a)	8. (d)	9. (b)	10. (c)
11. (b)	12. (a)	13. (c)	14. (c)	15. (d)
16. (a)	17. (c)	18. (b)	19. (c)	20. (b)
21. (c)	22. (b)	23. (a)	24. (c)	25. (b)
26. (b)	27. (c)	28. (a)	29. (c)	30. (c)
31. (d)	32. (b)	33. (c)	34. (c)	35. (d)
36. (c)	37. (a)	38. (c)	39. (b)	40. (c)
41. (a)	42. (b)	43. (d)	44. (c)	45. (a)
46. (a)	47. (d)	48. (b)	49. (b)	50. (c)
51. (a)	52. (c)	53. (b)	54. (a)	55. (c)
56. (b)	57. (d)	58. (b)		

Practice Set 10

1. Headquarter of 'IFLA' is located at :
   (a) Chicago (b) New York
   (c) London (d) The Hague
2. World of learning is :
   (a) A Dictionary (b) A Thesis
   (c) A Encyclopedia (d) An Abstracts
3. These documents are not primary sources :
   (a) Patents (b) Thesis
   (c) Conference Papers (d) Reference Books
4. National Library for visual handicapped is situated in:
   (a) New Delhi (b) Dehradun
   (c) London (d) New York
5. The first page of website is known as :
   (a) Title Page (b) Cover Page
   (c) Home Page (d) None of these
6. Blogs is a :
   (a) Internet Journal (b) Internet Abstract
   (c) E-book (d) Text Book
7. The owner of Internet is :
   (a) American Library Association
   (b) American Mathematical Society
   (c) American Scientist Group
   (d) None of the above
8. This literature is not published and not available through normal book selling channels :

(a) E-book (b) Journals
(c) Grey Literature (d) None of above

9. 'SCOPUS' is a :
(a) Full text database
(b) Abstracts and citation database
(c) Numerical database
(d) Alphabetical database

10. Handling of information in the sense of production is called :
(a) Information marketing
(b) Communication marketing
(c) Knowledge marketing
(d) Information revolution

11. Library as a living system "Takes a new matter, Costs off old matter, Changes in size and takes new shapes and term" whose quotation is this?
(a) C.A. Cutter (b) S.R. Ranganathan
(c) H.E. Bliss (d) Henry La Fountain

12. "NACLIN" is sponsored by :
(a) BONET (b) CALIBNET
(c) DELNET (d) INFLIBNET

13. Cataloguing-in-publication programme was first introduced by :
(a) National Library of UK
(b) The British Museum Library
(c) The British Library
(d) Library of Congress

14. The first Indian Storage Library was called :
(a) National Information Centre
(b) Indian National Documentation Centre

(c) Inter Library Resource Centre

(d) None of these

15. "WALFORD" guide to reference materials is a publication of :

(a) ALA (b) RRRLF

(c) UK and LA (d) ILA

16. "Choice of books is an unending work" whose quotation is this :

(a) C.A. Cutter (b) Melvil Dewey

(c) H.E. Bliss (d) Paul Outlet

17. The latest state, which enacted public library act is :

(a) Bihar (b) Arunachal Pradesh

(c) Goa (d) Uttar Pradesh

18. When was the Public Libraries Act Passed in Arunachal Pradesh?

(a) 2009 (b) 2008

(c) 2010 (d) 2013

19. When was the Public Libraries Act Passed in Rajasthan?

(a) 2013 (b) 2011

(c) 2008 (d) 2006

20. When was the Public Libraries Act Passed in Orissa?

(a) 2005 (b) 2003

(c) 2001 (d) 2008

21. The chronological sequence of the technology is :

(a) Television, Telephone, Satellite Communication, Internet

(b) Telephone, Television, Satellite Communication, Internet

(c) Internet, Satellite Communication, Telephone, Television

(d) None of these

22. Identify the correct order of the evolution of the following storage devices:
    (a) Pan drive, DVD, CD, Magnetic Tape
    (b) DVD, CD, Pan drive, Magnetic Tape
    (c) Magnetic Tape, Floppy, CD, DVD
    (d) None of these
23. Identify the correct order of evolution of computers :
    (a) Main Frame, Micro, PC-AT, AC-XT
    (b) PC-AT, AC-XT, Micro, Main Frame
    (c) Micro, PC-AT, Main Frame, AC-XT
    (d) None of these
24. Journal circulation can be of two type :
    (a) Vertical Radial Routing
    (b) Vertical and Routing
    (c) Circulation Routing and Radial Routing
    (d) None of these
25. The query "What is the address of American Embassy in India" include in :
    (a) Reference Service
    (b) Long Range Reference Service
    (c) Ready Reference Service
    (d) Translation Service
26. Which of the sequence is in ascending order ?
    (a) Terabytes, Gigabytes, Megabytes, Bytes
    (b) Gigabytes, Megabytes, Bytes, Terabytes
    (c) Megabytes, Bytes, Gigabytes, Terabytes
    (d) Bytes, Megabytes, Gigabytes, Terabytes
27. Which of the following would be the correct chronological sequence?

(a) Librametry, Bibliometrics, Informetrics, Webometrics

(b) Infometrics, Librametrics, Bibliometrics, Webometrics

(c) Bibliometrics, Infometrics, Librametrics, Webometrics

(d) None of these

28. 'Hypothesis' is a :

(a) Common Isolate (b) Cannon

(c) Speculation (d) Rule

29. A Hypothesis that is tested for its rejection is :

(a) Interview Hypothesis

(b) Research Hypothesis

(c) Observation Hypothesis

(d) Null Hypothesis

30. Mean, Median and Modes are :

(a) Way of things

(b) Measure of central tendency

(c) Both (a) and (b)

(d) None of these

31. The distinguishing features of digital devices are :

(a) Speech (b) Accuracy

(c) Both (a) and (b) (d) None of these

32. Analogue computers measure physical quantities because of :

(a) The Human Beings

(b) A Temperature and Accuracy

(c) Both (a) and (b)

(d) None of these

33. Digital computers assume more importance in applied information science because :
    (a) The capabilities for symbol manipulation
    (b) The capabilities for digital manipulation
    (c) The capabilities for information manipulation
    (d) The capabilities for knowledge manipulation
34. "Stock verification is a common practice in the following agencies only" choose the correct answer to justify it :
    (a) Libraries, government office and hospitals
    (b) Libraries, government office and residences
    (c) Libraries, government office and business houses
    (d) None of these
35. "Annual stock taking is usually done in order to assess profit and loss" choose the correct answer to justify it:
    (a) The statement is true
    (b) The statement is false
    (c) The statement is only true
    (d) None of these
36. Choose the correct answer from the following:
    (a) Stock articles are of permanent value
    (b) Stock articles are not permanent
    (c) Stock articles are consumables
    (d) None of these
37. Choose the correct answer from the following :
    (a) Casual leaves are subject to cumulation
    (b) Casual leaves are not subject to cumulation
    (c) Both (a) and (b)
    (d) None of these
38. Choose the right answer from the following :

(a) It is a consumable
(b) It is not a article
(c) It is not a stationary article
(d) None of these

39. System school of management is based on the following of :
(a) Ranganathan (b) Cutter
(c) Urwick (d) Tarry

40. "The high purpose of book selection is to provide the right book to the right reader at the right time". Whose quotation is this :
(a) Peter Drucker (b) Francis Drury
(c) H.E. Bliss (d) Milvil Dewey

41. "The wheat loan educational exchange programme" was initiated in :
(a) 1953 (b) 1951
(c) 1976 (d) 1980

42. Weeding of un-useful books from the library is emphasized by this law of library science :
(a) First laws of library science
(b) Second laws of library science
(c) Fourth laws of library science
(d) Fifth laws of library science

43. Identify the development in the following library software in correct chronological sequence:
(a) CDS/ISIS, SOUL, Green Stone, D-space
(b) SOUL, Green Stone, D-space, CDS/ISIS
(c) Green Stone, SOUL, D-space, CDS, ISIS
(d) D-space, CDS/ISIS, SOUL, Green Stone

44. What is meant by "Reinforced Binding"?

(a) Strengthening the book by supporting
(b) Strengthening the book by sewing
(c) Strengthening the book by adding some material
(d) None of these

45. What are different varieties of paper boards available today for binding of books?
(a) Grey boards (b) Milk board
(c) Straw boards (d) All of above

46. Who establishes contact of the users to the documents:
(a) Reference service
(b) Staff of the library
(c) Translation service
(d) Current Awareness Service

47. Now-a-days what is called to staff of the libraries?
(a) Human workers
(b) Reference services
(c) Library management
(d) Human resource

48. What is the main base of the library?
(a) Good reading materials collection
(b) Classification
(c) Library cataloguing
(d) Library management

49. What is the purpose of system analysis of the libraries?
(a) To remove and modify the faculty part
(b) To know the faculty part of the library
(c) To improve over the existing parts
(d) All of the above

50. Which type of filling order is used in LCSH for filling the entries?

(a) C.A. Cutters Rule
(b) ALA Rules
(c) Ranganathan's Rule
(d) Library of Congress Rules

51. In which year 'SLSH' was first published?
(a) 1923 (b) 1921
(c) 1927 (d) 1931

52. Chemical abstracts are published by whom?
(a) Cananian Chemica Society
(b) Indian Chemical Society
(c) American Chemical Society
(d) None of these

53. What is Chemical Abstracts?
(a) Translation Service (b) Referral Service
(c) Reference Service (d) Abstracting Service

54. What is the publication frequency of physics abstracts?
(a) Annualy (b) Weekly
(c) Fortnightly (d) Monthly

55. What is the meaning of the term "Profession"?
(a) Occupational operations executed with the help of others.
(b) Operations executed with the help of others
(c) Operations executed oneself
(d) None of these

56. Identify the chronological order of the following public libraries acts?
(a) Andhra Pradesh Public Libraries Act
(b) Maharashtra Public Libraries Act
(c) Karnataka Public Libraries Act
(d) First (a) Second (c) and Third (b)

57. Industrial environment in India is making a quantum jump because :
    (a) Information is a resource whose generation is money
    (b) Information absorptions and innovation in the field of the technology
    (c) Information is a resource that consumes money and time
    (d) None of these
58. Monopoly in business is coming to an end because of a :
    (a) Competitiveness (b) Money flow
    (c) Money less (d) Knowledge
59. Information is a must resource which :
    (a) Helps company to lose money
    (b) Helps company to achieve popularity
    (c) Helps company to have an edge in competition
    (d) None of these
60. The types of information usually sought by companies are :
    (a) Information on technology and market trends
    (b) Information on personnel relation
    (c) Economic and legal information
    (d) All of the above

ANSWERS

1. (d)	2. (a)	3. (d)	4. (b)	5. (c)
6. (a)	7. (d)	8. (c)	9. (b)	10. (a)
11. (b)	12. (c)	13. (d)	14. (c)	15. (c)
16. (a)	17. (b)	18. (a)	19. (d)	20. (c)
21. (b)	22. (c)	23. (a)	24. (c)	25. (c)
26. (d)	27. (a)	28. (c)	29. (d)	30. (b)
31. (c)	32. (b)	33. (a)	34. (c)	35. (b)
36. (a)	37. (b)	38. (c)	39. (c)	40. (b)
41. (b)	42. (d)	43. (a)	44. (c)	45. (d)
46. (b)	47. (d)	48. (a)	49. (d)	50. (b)
51. (a)	52. (c)	53. (d)	54. (c)	55. (a)
56. (d)	57. (b)	58. (a)	59. (b)	60. (d)

Practice Set 11

1. The London Library was founded in the year 1841 by:
   (a) Thomas Carlyle (b) Melvil Dewey
   (c) H.E. Bliss (d) C.A. Cutter
2. Which state enacted its Public Libraries Act in 1960?
   (a) Arunachal Pradesh (b) Uttar Pradesh
   (c) Madhya Pradesh (d) Andhra Pradesh
3. The public Library Management was started first from Baroda State in which year?
   (a) 1811 (b) 1910
   (c) 1915 (d) 1857
4. The British Museum Act was passed in the year :
   (a) 1750 (b) 1759
   (c) 1850 (d) 1911
5. 'Ranga' is the nickname of :
   (a) Ranganathan (b) Kesvan
   (c) Bhattacharya (d) Thakur
6. First ever Foreign Journey of Dr. S.R. Ranganathan was in the year :
   (a) 1924 (b) 1921
   (c) 1925 (d) 1927
7. In India working group on libraries was setup by :
   (a) Programming Commission
   (b) Planning Commission
   (c) Human Ministry Commission
   (d) None of these

8. William Allenson Borden was invited in India by :
   (a) National Library of India
   (b) Punjab University
   (c) Maharaja Syaji Rao Gaekwad III
   (d) Aligarh Muslim University
9. 'William Allenson Borden' was associated with Public Library Movement in :
   (a) Madras (b) Bihar
   (c) Maharashtra (d) Baroda
10. 'POSDCORB' coined by :
    (a) Peter Drucker (b) Luthar Gulic
    (c) George R Tarry (d) S.R. Ranganathan
11. Phyrr developed this technique:
    (a) Zero Based Budgeting
    (b) Line by Line Budgeting
    (c) Total Quality Management
    (d) Performance Budget
12. The unit for measuring the speed of the transmission of the data is called :
    (a) HTTP (b) Baud
    (c) RAM (d) ROM
13. Dublin core is related to :
    (a) CCF (b) ISBD
    (c) MARC (d) Metadata
14. "God has chosen me as an instrument, the honour done to me should act as an incentive to the generation to devote their lives whole heartedly to library science". Whose quotation is this?
    (a) Melvil Dewey (b) S.R. Ranganathan
    (c) H.E. Bliss (d) Henry La Fountain

15. Routing of Periodicals is considered as :
    (a) Current Awareness Service
    (b) Reference Service
    (c) Translation Service
    (d) Long Range Reference Service
16. A Statement that is to be tested in research is called :
    (a) Observation (b) Hypothesis
    (c) Research Design (d) Interview
17. 'ISDN' stands for :
    (a) International Standard Document Number
    (b) Indian Standard Document Number
    (c) International Standards Department Number
    (d) Integrated Service Digital Network
18. The following is the search engine for scientific information only :
    (a) Yahoo (b) Google
    (c) SCIRUS (d) Search Engine
19. One of the following has designed modals of communication :
    (a) Shannon of weaver (b) Dr. S.R. Ranganathan
    (c) Melvil Dewey (d) C.A. Cutter
20. 'OAI' stands for :
    (a) Open Access Information
    (b) Open Access Initiative
    (c) Open Archives Initiative
    (d) Open Access Informatics
21. Headquarters of 'UNESCO' is :
    (a) Paris (b) London
    (c) Mosco (d) New York

22. 'Search Strategy is the mirror in the dark'. Whose quotation is this?
    (a) Cutter (b) Ranganathan
    (c) KARTZ (d) Dewey
23. 'INDEST' is a :
    (a) Directory (b) Encyclopedia
    (c) Indexing (d) Consortium
24. 'ISBN' now consists of :
    (a) 15 digits (b) 13 digits
    (c) 16 digits (d) 10 digits
25. Which association was established in 1876?
    (a) Indian Library Association
    (b) Library Association, U.K.
    (c) American Library Association
    (d) Baroda State Library Association
26. Encyclopedia of library and information science is published by:
    (a) H.E. Bills (b) Marcal Dekkr
    (c) R.R Bowker (d) Colambia University
27. Boolean operator was derived by :
    (a) H.E. Bills (b) Hensie Boole
    (c) George Boole (d) None of these
28. In 'KWIC' Index, The keyword is :
    (a) Selected from the full text
    (b) Derived from the title
    (c) Assigned by the Author
    (d) None of these
29. The Term 'Subject Reference Code' is Related to ?
    (a) Broad System of ordering
    (b) Bibliographical Classified Scheme

(c) Colon Classification

(d) None of these

30. 'Bar Code' Technology is useful for :

(a) Circulation (b) Stock Taking

(c) Acquisition (d) All of the above

31. Now a Days much thought is given for :

(a) Broad based education

(b) Curriculum requirements

(c) Information scientists

(d) All of the above

32. Indian cannot afford to neglects of manpower training because :

(a) They are crucial to the success of development

(b) Of in sufficient provision of library schools

(c) They are not crucial for the success of development

(d) None of these

33. Specialized information science education institutes produce better professionals as :

(a) They do not have good curricula

(b) They have better curricula and infrastructure

(c) Both (a) and (b)

(d) None of these

34. LIS education is now pertinent to :

(a) Reduce the curricula

(b) Have status quo in curricula

(c) Design curricula

(d) Fallow exiting curricula

35. Training for librarianship must be at per :

(a) With the present set up

(b) With the previous set up

(c) With the old set up

(d) With the future set up

36. Which is the primary source for finding out periodicals in agriculture?

(a) Reference Asia

(b) Ulrich International Periodical Directory

(c) Press in India

(d) Publication in India

37. Which of the following indexes only paper presented in the conferences?

(a) LIS

(b) LISA

(c) ISIP

(d) Current Research Abstracts

38. Appropriate Communication Media for CD-Net is :

(a) Optical Cable (b) Optical Fiber

(c) Optical Disk (d) Twisted Wires

39. 'IATLIS' is an association of :

(a) Special Libraries

(b) Public Libraries

(c) Library Science Faculty

(d) None of these

40. Identify the association that has changed its original name :

(a) Indian library Association

(b) Library Association

(c) American Library Association

(d) British Library Association

41. Recall and Precision Ratio are used in the evaluation of :

(a) Communication Retrieval
(b) Information Retrieval
(c) Current Awareness Service
(d) Biographical Service

42. 'Emerold' is the database of :
(a) Library and information Science Literature
(b) Information Communication
(c) Knowledge Communication
(d) Material Science Literature

43. 'TQM' was promulgamated by :
(a) Maslow (b) Deming and Juran
(c) Ranganathan (d) Peter Drucker

44. 'MeSH' is the name of a :
(a) Job Analysis (b) Controlled Vocabulary
(c) Research Database (d) None of these

45. 'Rules for Dictionary Catalogue' was devised by :
(a) Melvil Dewey (b) H.E. Bliss
(c) C.A. Cutter (d) S.R. Ranganathan

46. Management is an example of how knowledge grow by :
(a) Fusion (b) Distillation
(c) Lamination (d) None of these

47. 'Dichotomy Classification' is also known as :
(a) Binary Classification (b) Colon Classification
(c) Bias Classification (d) Subject Classification

48. Phoenix Schedule means :
(a) Almost Faceted
(b) Rigidly Faceted
(c) A completely new development of the schedule for a specific discipline
(d) None of these

49. Retroactive ordinal notation invented by :
    (a) S.R. Ranganathan (b) H.E. Bliss
    (c) Henry La Fountain (d) Melvil Dewey
50. The shelf list in the library is to facilitate :
    (a) Library cess (b) Library acquisition
    (c) Stock verification (d) Library finance
51. Invitation on quotations is done at the :
    (a) Preorder work
    (b) Order placing work
    (c) Supply receiving work
    (d) None of these
52. Annual Report of the Library is usually having two parts namely :
    (a) Library Service
    (b) Descriptive and Statistical
    (c) Library Staff
    (d) Technical Service
53. The library statistics usually pertains to library resources, technical service and :
    (a) Library staff (b) User's service
    (c) Library budget (d) Library finance
54. 'BC' stands for :
    (a) Bibliographical classes
    (b) Biological Class
    (c) Bibliographic Classification
    (d) None of these
55. In DDC 19th edition, the notation of table 03 and table 04 mainly are applicable only to their respective main classes :

(a) Sociological Science
(b) Study and Teachings
(c) Dictionaries
(d) Literatures and Languages

56. Which edition of 'DDC' is available in CD-ROM :
(a) 16th edition (b) 21st edition
(c) 19th edition (d) 20th edition

57. In DDC 21st edition the synthesis is achieved through the use of :
(a) Seven Tables and Add to instructions
(b) Summaries
(c) Index
(d) Schedule

58. In the first edition of "Colon Classification" (CC), which connecting symbol was used :
(a) Comma (,) (b) Colon (:)
(c) Semi-colon (;) (d) Dot (.)

59. In which university S.R. Ranganathan worked as a professor of library science from 1947 – 1955?
(a) Madras University
(b) Banaras Hindu University
(c) Patna University
(d) Delhi University

60. S.R. Ranganathan was university librarian and professor of library science at Banaras Hindu University (BHU) in year to :
(a) 1940-1943 (b) 1942-1945
(c) 1945-1947 (d) 1946-1948

ANSWERS

1. (a)	2. (d)	3. (b)	4. (b)	5. (b)
6. (a)	7. (b)	8. (c)	9. (d)	10. (b)
11. (a)	12. (b)	13. (d)	14. (b)	15. (a)
16. (b)	17. (d)	18. (c)	19. (a)	20. (c)
21. (a)	22. (c)	23. (d)	24. (b)	25. (c)
26. (b)	27. (c)	28. (b)	29. (a)	30. (d)
31. (d)	32. (a)	33. (b)	34. (c)	35. (a)
36. (b)	37. (c)	38. (b)	39. (c)	40. (b)
41. (b)	42. (a)	43. (b)	44. (b)	45. (c)
46. (b)	47. (a)	48. (c)	49. (b)	50. (c)
51. (a)	52. (b)	53. (b)	54. (c)	55. (d)
56. (b)	57. (a)	58. (b)	59. (d)	60. (c)

Practice Set 12

1. The term "Yellow Journalism" refers to :
   (a) Sensationalism and exaggeration to attract readers
   (b) Sensationalism news print in yellow paper
   (c) Sensationalism news about arts and culture
   (d) None of these
2. In the classroom, the teacher sends the massage either as words or image. The students are really :
   (a) Dynamic (b) Encoders
   (c) Decoders (d) None of these
3. Media is known as :
   (a) Third State (b) Fourth State
   (c) Five State (d) Six State
4. The mode of communication that involves a single source transmitting information to a llarge number of receivers simultaneously, is called :
   (a) Internet Communication
   (b) Group Communication
   (c) Information Communication
   (d) Mass Communication
5. A smart classroom is a teaching space which has :
   (a) Projector and Screen
   (b) Smart portion with a touch panel control system
   (c) PC/laptop connection and DVD/VCR player
   (d) All of the above
6. Digital empowerment means :

(a) Universal Digital Literacy
(b) Universal Access to all Digital Resources
(c) Both (a) and (b)
(d) None of these

7. The next term in the Series :
2, 7, 28, 63, 126, ...
(a) 215 (b) 220
(c) 216 (d) 219

8. The next term in the series :
AB, ED, IH, NM, ...
(a) SU (b) TS
(c) CA (d) ST

9. If 'STREAMERS' is coded as 'UVTGALDQR' then 'KNOWLEDGE' will be coded as :
(a) PMQLYCDFD (b) MPQLYCDFD
(c) MPSYLDCFD (d) None of these

10. A is brother of B, B is the brother of C, C is the husband of D, E is the father of A, D is related to E as :
(a) Daughter-in-law (b) Sister-in-law
(c) Brother-in-law (d) Father-in-law

11. 'FAQ' stands for :
(a) Frequently Asked Question
(b) Frequently as a Question
(c) Frequently Access Question
(d) Frequently Added Question

12. Internet explorer is a :
(a) Search engine (b) Application software
(c) Client software (d) Server software

13. 'SOUL' software based on :

(a) HTTP (b) SQL-Server 7.0
(c) C++ (d) FORTRAN

14. Which of the following is a translator programme:
(a) Compiler (b) Assembler
(c) Interpreter (d) All of the above

15. Which language use pointer :
(a) C (b) Basic
(c) General (d) COBOL

16. Which of the following is web browser :
(a) Netscape navigator
(b) Microsoft Internet Exporer
(c) Both (a) and (b)
(d) None of these

17. The classified catalogue is a :
(a) Subject Catalogue (b) Title Catalogue
(c) Author Catalogue (d) Translator Catalogue

18. The two prominent inner forms of catalogues are :
(a) Numerical Catalogue
(b) Alphabetical Catalogue and Classes Catalogue
(c) Classified Catalogue and Dictionary Catalogue
(d) None of these

19. In the directing section of the class index entry in CCC, the last link is followed by the :
(a) Call Number (b) Class Number
(c) Collection Number (d) Stock Number

20. When a publisher provides the catalogue entry in the book itself, it is known as :
(a) Catalogue entry
(b) Subject catalogue

(c) Cataloguing in source
(d) Book trade catalogue

21. Which one is the first law of library science enunciated by S.R. Ranganathan?
(a) Books are for use
(b) Save the time of the reader
(c) Every reader his book
(d) Every book his reader

22. Why "Wadia Committee' (1967) was set up?
(a) University library
(b) College library
(c) New techniques of library training
(d) None of these

23. Who was the chairman of Library Advisory Committee (1957)?
(a) S.R. Ranganathan (b) Kesavan
(c) Kothari (d) K.P. Sinha

24. The 'working group of libraries' was set up by whom to study about the libraries in India?
(a) Human Right Commission
(b) Planning Commission
(c) Education Council
(d) University Grant Commission

25. Which one is the most suitable source for finding out background of Ajanta Arts?
(a) Encyclopedia (b) Dictionary
(c) Hand Book (d) Annual Report

26. Which organization has been mainly providing translation services in India?
(a) UNISIST (b) INSDOC
(c) DESIDOC (d) SENDOC

27. 'INSDOC' translates cover to cover translation of which language?
(a) French (b) Urdu
(c) Russian (d) English

28. When 'European Translation Centre' was established in ?
(a) 1930 (b) 1951
(c) 1962 (d) 1957

29. Where is the Headquarter of European Translation Centre?
(a) Rome (b) Delft
(c) Chicago (d) New York

30. When 'NTC' was established in USA?
(a) 1949 (b) 1953
(c) 1956 (d) 1960

31. When 'IFLA' convened on international meeting of experts in copenhagon?
(a) 1965 (b) 1976
(c) 1972 (d) 1969

32. Who is the chairman of "National Knowledge Commission"?
(a) Sam Pitroda (b) Kalpna Chawala
(c) Manmohan Singh (d) Rahul Boss

33. What year was "National Knowledge Commission" Formed?
(a) 16th January 2004 (b) 13th June 2005
(c) 19th February 2001 (d) 12th August 2006

34. Which of the following indexing only paper presented in the conference?
(a) Research in progress (b) LISA
(c) ISTP (d) None of these

35. "National Knowledge Commission" was established during the rule of which prime minister?
    (a) Chaudhary Charan Singh
    (b) Atal Bihari Vajpai
    (c) Dr. Manmohan Singh
    (d) Narendra Modi
36. The following system can survive in isolation :
    (a) Accounting System
    (b) Planning System
    (c) Inventory Management System
    (d) No System
37. It anyone wants information from two systems, he must get the information:
    (a) From Two Systems and Need not Correlation
    (b) From One System at a Time for Correlation
    (c) From each System and Correlate
    (d) None of these
38. All the systems must be integrated for :
    (a) Dramatic Impact (b) Isolation
    (c) Proper Planning (d) None of these
39. Collecting and Arranging data is :
    (a) Needed for production planning
    (b) Needed for Library Personnel
    (c) Needed for Functioning Department
    (d) All of the Above
40. The executives and managers cannot make good decisions :
    (a) Only when they collect the data themselves
    (b) With the isolated data
    (c) Both (a) and (b)
    (d) None of these

41. Who has not changed its name ?
    (a) American Library Association (ALA)
    (b) Library Association (UK)
    (c) Developing Library Network, India
    (d) IFLA
42. Which of the following is not correct?
    (a) Theory 'Z' is the contribution of Japanese style of management
    (b) Mission of an organization is essentially abstract
    (c) Money is the most powerful motivation agent
    (d) None of these
43. 'NISCAIR' is a part of :
    (a) DRDO (b) UGC
    (c) CSIR (d) ISRO
44. Use of microfilming is considerably reduced due to :
    (a) Need for use microfilm reader
    (b) Availability of better technology in the form of digitization
    (c) High cost involved in it
    (d) All of the above
45. OPAQUE paper is a :
    (a) Transparent Paper (b) None Transparent Paper
    (c) Ultra White Paper (d) None of these
46. Which of the following is a public domain database :
    (a) MEDLARS (b) INIS
    (c) AGRIS (d) UNESCO
47. One of the following journals is published in 'U.K.'?
    (a) Program (b) Library Annual
    (c) Library Quarterly (d) Library Weekly

48. Fair use is a term most relevant to :
   (a) Public Library Act
   (b) Copyright
   (c) Use of Reference Books
   (d) None of these

49. Which of the following does not fall into the category of pre-coordinate indexing?
   (a) Chain Indexing
   (b) Subject Indexing
   (c) Uniform Indexing
   (d) Library of Congress Subject Headings

50. Which of the following is not associated with communication system?
   (a) Sender (b) Receiver
   (c) Channel (d) Entropy

51. 'DESIDOC' is documentation centre for :
   (a) Defense Science (b) Library Science
   (c) Chemistry Science (d) Rural Development

52. Mean, median and mode are :
   (a) Measure of deviation
   (b) Ways of sampling
   (c) Measures of control tendency
   (d) None of the above

53. Cornfield studies are an example of :
   (a) Historical Research (b) Experimental Research
   (c) Primary Research (d) Survey Research

54. Which factors force organization to use 'IT' to names information?
   (a) Availability of latest information on real time basis

(b) Time, Value and complex nature of information on real time basis

(c) Explosion of sources of information

(d) None of these

55. Major obstacle in taking accurate futuristic decisions is :

(a) Cut throat completion

(b) Availability of more information

(c) Both (a) and (b)

(d) None of these

56. Which is the most appropriate tool to make better use of information?

(a) Information Technology

(b) Communication Technology

(c) Computer Technology

(d) None of these

57. What are critical characteristics of information delivery system for making its use effective?

(a) Developing Quality Photocopying and fax facility

(b) Right information delivered at right time

(c) Ability to develop appropriate information products

(d) All of the above

58. What is the crucial decision for an organization to take to beat the competition?

(a) To establish a separate development for acquiring and processing

(b) To strengthen the libraries already existing in the organization

(c) To create a mechanism to access, organize and process

(d) None of these

59. "Connemara Public Library" is situated at :

(a) Chennai (b) Baroda

(c) Delhi (d) Kolkata

60. 'GOC' was constituted in year :

(a) 1976 (b) 1966

(c) 1965 (d) 1971

ANSWERS

1. (a)	2. (c)	3. (b)	4. (d)	5. (d)
6. (c)	7. (a)	8. (b)	9. (c)	10. (a)
11. (a)	12. (c)	13. (b)	14. (d)	15. (a)
16. (c)	17. (a)	18. (c)	19. (b)	20 (c)
21. (a)	22. (c)	23. (d)	24. (b)	25. (a)
26. (b)	27. (c)	28. (a)	29. (b)	30. (b)
31. (d)	32. (a)	33. (b)	34. (a)	35. (c)
36. (d)	37. (c)	38. (a)	39. (c)	40. (b)
41. (a)	42. (c)	43. (c)	44. (d)	45. (b)
46. (c)	47. (a)	48. (b)	49. (c)	50. (d)
51. (a)	52. (c)	53. (b)	54. (c)	55. (b)
56. (a)	57. (b)	58. (c)	59. (a)	60. (d)

Practice Set 13

1. "Traits de Documentation" was brought out by 'Paul Otlet' in :
   (a) 1942 (b) 1931
   (c) 1934 (d) 1925
2. Preparation, Service and Assimilation are the main stages involved in :
   (a) Reference Service
   (b) User Education
   (c) Translation Service
   (d) Current Awareness Service
3. Which of the following is not a form of 'CAS'?
   (a) Library Journals
   (b) Select Dessimination Information
   (c) Indexing Periodicals
   (d) Library Bulletine
4. Computerised 'SDI' comes in :
   (a) 1957 (b) 1956
   (c) 1959 (d) 1961
5. 'ORBIT' was developed in :
   (a) 1960 (b) 1968
   (c) 1961 (d) 1971
6. 'CODEN' was developed by :
   (a) American Society for Testing and Materials
   (b) Canadian Chemical Society
   (c) Indian Chemical Society
   (d) None of these

7. The International Centre for registration of serials was setup in :
   (a) 1975 (b) 1971
   (c) 1967 (d) 1969
8. 'NADC' programme is related to :
   (a) Library cess
   (b) Equisition
   (c) Co-operation Cataloguing
   (d) Library management
9. 'BNB' adopted which of the following for preparing subject index?
   (a) KWIC (b) INDEXING
   (c) POPSI (d) PRECIS
10. The first edition of CC (Colon Classification) was published in year :
    (a) 1933 (b) 1931
    (c) 1934 (d) 1939
11. The quotation where is the wisdom, we lost in knowledge is by :
    (a) T.S. Eliot (b) H.E. Bliss
    (c) George R. Tarry (d) None of these
12. Entropy is a measure of :
    (a) Degree of relevant of information
    (b) Degree of uncertainty in information
    (c) Degree of certainty in information
    (d) All the above
13. CONPOLIS (India) was setup in the year :
    (a) 1976 (b) 1991
    (c) 1988 (d) 1985
14. First time efforts for the development of libraries in

India were made :

(a) B.S. Kesavan
(b) G. Bhattacharya
(c) Sayaji Rao Gaekwad III
(d) S.R. Ranganathan

15. An E-book which does not require and internet connection to access its contents is :

(a) Printed Book (b) Digital Book
(c) Hand Written Book (d) Electronic Book

16. Emerald Full Text Database is published from :

(a) USA (b) Canada
(c) France (d) United Kingdom (UK)

17. Who propounded "Conservative Moderate and Liberal Theories of Reference Service"?

(a) James I. Wyer (b) S.R. Ranganathan
(c) C.A. Cutter (d) Henry La Fountain

18. The input centre for 'INIS' in India is :

(a) INSDOC (b) DESIDOC
(c) DRDO (d) BARC

19. The provision of phase relation in 'DDC' was made available from :

(a) 19th edition (b) 11th edition
(c) 15th edition (d) 20th edition

20. RDA stands for :

(a) Reference Describe Analysis
(b) Reference Description Analysis
(c) Resource Description and Access
(d) Reference Department Agency

21. Cost benefit analysis means :

(a) Performance evaluation based on cost

(b) Performance evaluation based on inputs
(c) Performance evaluation based on outputs
(d) None of these

22. Which "National Agency in India" is assigning the ISBN?
(a) National Library of India
(b) Delhi Public Library
(c) National Information Centre
(d) Raja Ram Mohan Roy National Education Resource Centre

23. The term 'Cyberspace' was first used by :
(a) Joe Flower (b) H.E. Bliss
(c) Wiliam Gibson (d) John Postall

24. What is the 'Notation' of 'DDC' classification method?
(a) Pure (b) Mixed
(c) Do not know (d) None of these

25. What is the 'Notation' of 'CC' classification method?
(a) Pure (b) Mixed
(c) Do not know (d) None of these

26. Two kind of main memory are :
(a) RAM (b) ROM
(c) Both (a) and (b) (d) None of these

27. Pascal Addition Machine was invented in year :
(a) 1936 (b) 1942
(c) 1957 (d) 1931

28. Select the Micro Computer :
(a) CDS-205 (b) ANURAG
(c) IBM PS/2 (d) None of these

29. Floppies are most commonly used media with :

(a) Micro Computer (b) Mini Computer
(c) Super Computer (d) Main Frame Computer

30. The user can enter the data through :
(a) Mouse (b) Key Board
(c) Both (a) and (b) (d) None of these

31. 'INTXT' project was launched by :
(a) Doordarshan and NIC
(b) Doordarshan and JNC
(c) Doordarshan and IGNOL
(d) None of these

32. The Boolean Operator 'ADD' is related to :
(a) Logical Difference (b) Practical Difference
(c) Productive (d) Additive

33. The process of configuring the disks into tracks and sectors is called :
(a) Booting (b) Labeling
(c) Formatting (d) All of above

34. A Research Design is :
(a) A series of guide posts
(b) A series of sampling
(c) Both (a) and (b)
(d) None of these

35. In a questionnaire, questionnaire on age, income and gender are the example of :
(a) Dependent variable
(b) Independent variables
(c) Manipulation variables
(d) None of these

36. The simple Dublin Core Metadata Element Set (DCMES) consists of :

(a) 19 elements (b) 18 elements

(c) 10 elements (d) 15 elements

37. 'Libraries as Gateways to Knowledge is the time of the document :

(a) National Knowledge Commission on Libraries, 2007

(b) National Information Policy, 1986

(c) Information Technology Act, 2000

(d) University Grant Commission, 1956

38. Rolland Munro described accountability as :

(a) Formal Artifacts only

(b) Informal, formal and documentary records

(c) Classified documentary artifacts

(d) None of these

39. The phrase 'Record Keeping' is associated with :

(a) Computer Software (b) Computer Programmes

(c) Archivists (d) Office Managers

40. What Integral Components Munro has Identified for accounting in the business?

(a) Records and Code (b) Materials and Devices

(c) Legal Regulations (d) All of the above

41. In which year was the 'Madras Library Association' (MLA) established :

(a) 1928 (b) 1926

(c) 1924 (d) 1921

42. In which year was the 'Karnataka Library Association' (KLA) established :

(a) 1926 (b) 1929

(c) 1927 (d) 1933

43. In which year was the 'Indian Library Association' established :

(a) 1936 (b) 1938
(c) 1929 (d) 1933

44. In which year was the 'Special Library Association (UK)' established:
(a) 1899 (b) 1890
(c) 1909 (d) 1910

45. In which year was the 'Association for Management' established :
(a) 1926 (b) 1924
(c) 1940 (d) 1942

46. In which year was the 'UNESCO' established :
(a) 1946 (b) 1948
(c) 1936 (d) 1942

47. An invisible college is a typical example of :
(a) Arrangement channel of communication
(b) Formal Channel of communication
(c) Informal channel of communication
(d) None of these

48. Berne Convention was adopted in the year :
(a) 1910 (b) 1899
(c) 1886 (d) 1942

49. 'FID' was dissolved in the year :
(a) 2001 (b) 2006
(c) 2008 (d) 2002

50. Which source would you consult to get latest information on controversies about the venue for Tata's Nano?
(a) India : A Reference Annual
(b) New Encyclopedia Britannica
(c) Asian Recorder
(d) None of these

51. 'Buble Link' is a :
    (a) MARC (b) OPAC
    (c) CCF (d) Subject Gateway
52. Who has given the minimal, middling and maximum theory of reference service?
    (a) C.A. Cutter (b) S.R. Ranganathan
    (c) Samuel Rothstein (d) None of these
53. 'Compaction' is an important feature of :
    (a) Indexes (b) Reviews
    (c) Bibliographies (d) Biography
54. 'Geophysics' has been formed as a result of :
    (a) Fussion (b) Acquisition
    (c) Lamination (d) All the above
55. Which one is not a canon (as given Ranganathan) :
    (a) Canon of Currency
    (b) Canon of Comprehensiveness
    (c) Canon of Context
    (d) None of these
56. 'ZBB' was developed by :
    (a) Peter A Phyrr (b) Peter Drucker
    (c) George R. Tarry (d) C.A. Cutter
57. 'PERT' was developed by :
    (a) Booz Alean Hamelton
    (b) The Navy Special Project Office
    (c) INIS
    (d) UNESCO
58. The term hypertext was coined by :
    (a) Billgates (b) Charles Babbage
    (c) Ted Nelson (d) None of these

59. The 12 Rules for Relational Database were given by :
(a) Tay Vaughan (b) Time Berner Lee
(c) J. Bill Gates (d) Edgar F. Codd

60. The Complete Bibliographic details in MARC are available in :
(a) Control Field (b) Variable Field
(c) Record Directing (d) All of the above

ANSWERS

1. (c)	2. (a)	3. (c)	4. (c)	5. (b)
6. (a)	7. (b)	8. (c)	9. (d)	10. (a)
11. (a)	12. (b)	13. (d)	14. (c)	15. (b)
16. (d)	17. (a)	18. (d)	19. (b)	20. (c)
21. (a)	22. (d)	23. (c)	24. (a)	25. (b)
26. (c)	27. (b)	28. (c)	29. (a)	30. (c)
31. (a)	32. (d)	33. (c)	34. (a)	35. (b)
36. (d)	37. (a)	38. (b)	39. (c)	40. (b)
41. (a)	42. (b)	43. (d)	44. (c)	45. (b)
46. (a)	47. (c)	48. (c)	49. (d)	50. (a)
51. (d)	52. (c)	53. (b)	54. (a)	55. (b)
56. (a)	57. (b)	58. (c)	59. (d)	60. (a)

Practice Set 14

1. 'INIS' is an information system programme of :
   (a) IAEA
   (b) UNESCO
   (c) Atomic Energy Commission
   (d) World Atomic Energy Consortia
2. 'EMIS' was created by :
   (a) UNESCO
   (b) INIS
   (c) Atomic Energy Commission
   (d) European Commission on Atomic Energy
3. 'EMIS' stands for :
   (a) European material Information Service
   (b) Electronic Material Information Service
   (c) Electronics Material Information System
   (d) None of these
4. 'Index Medicus' published since :
   (a) 1910 (b) 1886
   (c) 1879 (d) 1898
5. 'INIS – Atom Index' was first published in :
   (a) 1981 (b) 1976
   (c) 1969 (d) 1970
6. 'MEDLARS-II' started in :
   (a) 1978 (b) 1975
   (c) 1973 (d) 1971

7. Conversion of Barcode in to electrical signals is done by :
   (a) Scanners (b) Photo Sensor
   (c) Unicode (d) None of these
8. Bibliographic Coupling was first advocate by :
   (a) George R. Tarry (b) Peter Drucker
   (c) M.M. Kessler (d) S.C. Brodford
9. External and Internal criticism implies in :
   (a) Applied Research (b) Historical Research
   (c) Primary Research (d) Survey Research
10. Granthana is an official publication of :
   (a) Indian Library Association
   (b) IASLIC
   (c) Information Library Network (INFLIBNET)
   (d) Raja Ram Mohan Roy Library Foundation (RRRLF)
11. Million Book Project was initiated by :
   (a) Carnegie Melon University
   (b) Chicago University
   (c) London University
   (d) New York University
12. When special library association was setup in 'USA':
   (a) 1910 (b) 1909
   (c) 1911 (d) 1917
13. 'IASLIC' is an Association of which type of libraries?
   (a) Academic Library (b) Public Library
   (c) College Library (d) Special Library
14. Which of the following library association was setup first at state level?

(a) Madras Library Association

(b) Bihar Library Association

(c) Karnataka Library Association

(d) Andhra Pradesh Library Association

15. What is full name of 'IASLIC'?

(a) International Association of School Library Centre

(b) International Association of Special Library Centre

(c) International Association of Special Library and Information Centre

(d) Indian Association of Special Libraries and Information Centre

16. Which organization introduced 'COMPASS' Indexing system?

(a) BNB (b) INB

(c) ISSN (d) ISBN

17. 'LCSH' stands for :

(a) Library of Congress Subject Headings

(b) Library Classification of Subject Headings

(c) Library Cataloguing of Subject Headings

(d) None of these

18. Who developed Classaurus?

(a) B.S. Kesavan (b) Ganesh Bhattacharya

(c) Peter Drucker (d) S.R. Ranganathan

19. The principles of Library Management are the same to the principle of :

(a) Personal Management

(b) Library Management

(c) Business Management

(d) School Library Management

20. What is meant by System Analysis?

(a) Study of the system by analyzing its components
(b) Analysis of the components of the system
(c) Both (a) and (b)
(d) None of these

21. Which one using ISSN?
(a) British National Bibliography
(b) Indian National Bibliography
(c) Ulrich International Periodical Directory
(d) None of these

22. "Education is the manifestation of perfection already in man" was started by :
(a) Swami Vivekanand
(b) Mahatma Gandhi
(c) Swami Dayanand Saraswati
(d) Ravindra Nath Tagore

23. Which of the following is not a prescribed level of teaching?
(a) Reflective (b) Differentiation
(c) Memory (d) None of these

24. Maximum participation of student during teaching is possible through :
(a) Sampling method (b) Demonstration method
(c) Survey method (d) Lectural method

25. Diagnostic evaluation ascertains :
(a) Student performance of the beginning of instructions
(b) Degree of achievement of instructions of the end
(c) Causes and remedies of persistent learning problems during instructions
(d) All of these

26. Instructional aids are used by the teacher to :
    (a) Ensure discipline (b) Clarify the concepts
    (c) Both (a) and (b) (d) None of these
27. Attitude of the teacher that effects teaching pertains to :
    (a) Cognitive Domain (b) Connecting Domain
    (c) Connative Domain (d) Affective Domain
28. Which of the following powers the president has in relation to 'Lok Sabha'?
    (a) Summoning (b) Adjournment - Sine die
    (c) Prorogation (d) Both (a) and (c)
29. The interval between two sessions of parliament must not exceed :
    (a) 6 Months (b) 8 Months
    (c) 5 Months (d) 12 Months
30. Right to privacy as a fundamental right is implied in :
    (a) Right equality
    (b) Right to freedom
    (c) Right to life and personal liberty
    (d) None of these
31. Which of the following organizations deals with "Capacity Building Program" on Educational Planning?
    (a) RRRLF (b) NUEPA
    (c) DELNET (d) IFLIBNET
32. The cyclone 'Hudhud' hit the coast of which state :
    (a) Karnataka (b) Kerala
    (c) Madras (d) Goa
33. Which of the following is not a renewable natural resource?

(a) Soil (b) Water
(c) Air (d) Salt

34. The maximum number of fake institutions has identified by the UGC in the year 2014 are in the state/ union territory of :
(a) Uttar Pradesh (b) Madhya Pradesh
(c) New Delhi (d) Bihar

35. Which of the following institutions are empowered to confer or grant degrees under the UGC Act, 1956?
(a) A university established by an act of parliament
(b) A university established by an act of legislature
(c) An institution which is a deemed to be university
(d) All of the above

36. The policy makers of Brazil are primarily concerned with :
(a) Impact of liberalizations an IT use and product
(b) Instability of Brazilian politics
(c) Both (a) and (b)
(d) None of these

37. What are the professional skills required to meet the global market?
(a) Skilled suitable and global needs
(b) Unskilled, suitable to local labour needs
(c) Highly skilled suitable to local needs
(d) None of these

38. What was the significance of "Green House Policy" of Brazil?
(a) Investment in the social sector
(b) Investment in the IT sector
(c) Investment in the banking sector,
(d) Investment in the environmental sector

39. Effects of customization in different sectors of Brazilian industry are :
    (a) Diffusion of 'IT' in line with local needs
    (b) Attracting new foreign direct investment
    (c) Development of local industry
    (d) None of these
40. What is the driving force that attracted foreign investment in Brazil?
    (a) Adoption of Green House Policy
    (b) Organised and Automated Banking Sector
    (c) Industrial Capacity and Skilled Work Force
    (d) None of these
41. Who expressed knowledge in a simple mathematical equation K(S) + V1 = K(S + VS)?
    (a) B.C. Brooks (b) Shannon and Viber
    (c) L.M. Sharma (d) None of these
42. Which is not a near synonym term to information?
    (a) Classification (b) Catalogue
    (c) Information (d) Knowledge
43. Resource sharing among libraries was prompted by the factors :
    (a) Price escalation (b) Information explosion
    (c) Both (a) and (b) (d) None of these
44. The Library Association (UK) is now the component of :
    (a) CILIP (b) ASLIM
    (c) IASLIC (d) RRRLF
45. Which of the following professionals associations does not exist now ?
    (a) ALA (b) IASLIC
    (c) FID (d) ILA

46. Real Time Access refers to :
    (a) Access in Advance
    (b) Access after some time
    (c) Both (a) and (b)
    (d) Access when searched for

47. 'Dewey Decimal Classification (DDC)' is now looked after by :
    (a) ALA (b) MEDLARS
    (c) UNESCO (d) OCLC

48. 'World Wide Web' (WWW) was first designed by :
    (a) Tim Berner's Lee (b) H.P. Luhn
    (c) F.W. Lancaster (d) Charles Babbage

49. A type of indexing where term are coordinated prior to searching :
    (a) Uniterm Indexing
    (b) Subject Indexing
    (c) Pre Coordinate Indexing
    (d) Post Coordinate Indexing

50. Use of Integrated Circuits was made in :
    (a) First Generation Computer
    (b) Third Generation Computer
    (c) Fourth Generation Computer
    (d) Second Generation Computer

51. The Network Topology in which nodes are connected to a central hub is known as:
    (a) Hub topology (b) Star topology
    (c) Ring topology (d) Bus topology

52. Which of the following is a term used for working assumption of a solution to a problem?
    (a) Hypothesis (b) Observation

(c) Interview (d) Bibliography

53. Computer memory is measured in :
    (a) Bytes (b) Megabytes
    (c) Kilobytes (d) All of the above

54. 'CCF' stands for :
    (a) Classified Catalogue Format
    (b) Colon Classification Format
    (c) Common Communication Format
    (d) Computer Classification Format

55. 'DRDO' stands for :
    (a) Department of Research
    (b) Defense Research and Description Organisation
    (c) Defense Research and Development Organisation
    (d) None of these

56. 'NASA' stands for:
    (a) National Aeronautics and Space Administration
    (b) National Atomic Space Administration
    (c) National Atomic System Administration
    (d) None of these

57. 'ILA' stands for :
    (a) International Library Association
    (b) Indian Library Association
    (c) Indian Library Standards
    (d) None of these

58. 'ISRO' stands for :
    (a) Indian Space Research Organisation
    (b) International Space Research Organisation
    (c) Indian System for Research Organisation
    (d) None of these

59. 'INSDOC' stands for :
    (a) Indian National Scientific Development Centre
    (b) Indian National Science Documentation Centre
    (c) Indian National Scientific Documentation Centre
    (d) None of these
60. 'CSIR' stands for :
    (a) Council of Scientific and Industrial Research
    (b) Council of Science and Indian Research
    (c) Council of Science and International Research
    (d) None of these

ANSWERS

1. (a)	2. (b)	3. (b)	4. (c)	5. (d)
6. (b)	7. (a)	8. (c)	9. (b)	10. (d)
11. (a)	12. (b)	13. (d)	14. (a)	15. (d)
16. (a)	17. (a)	18. (b)	19. (c)	20. (b)
21. (c)	22. (a)	23. (b)	24. (b)	25. (c)
26. (b)	27. (d)	28. (d)	29. (a)	30. (c)
31. (b)	32. (b)	33. (d)	34. (a)	35. (d)
36. (a)	37. (c)	38. (b)	39. (a)	40. (c)
41. (a)	42. (b)	43. (c)	44. (a)	45. (c)
46. (d)	47. (d)	48. (a)	49. (c)	50. (b)
51. (b)	52. (a)	53. (d)	54. (c)	55. (c)
56. (a)	57. (b)	58. (a)	59. (c)	60. (a)

Practice Set 15

1. What is an invention?
   (a) It is the idea that has the characteristics of application
   (b) A process benefits
   (c) A process bereft of use
   (d) None of these
2. In invention involves?
   (a) Simply on efforts to explore past knowledge
   (b) Redefining knowledge of the past
   (c) Exploiting past knowledge and newly collected facts
   (d) None of these
3. Industrial development and competitive environment are possible when :
   (a) Invention lead to innovation
   (b) Invention follows innovation
   (c) Invention prevents innovation
   (d) Invention has little practical innovation
4. Invention is carried out at present ?
   (a) By industrialist to achieves success in business
   (b) By an individual researcher when high level imagination
   (c) Both (a) and (b)
   (d) None of these
5. What is innovation?

(a) Innovation is a theoretical process
(b) Innovation is a process of application of invention
(c) Innovation provides data for invention
(d) All of the above

6. According to Machlup the Difference between Information and Knowledge is :
(a) Information is piecemeal, fragmented, particular whereas knowledge is structured, coherent and universal
(b) Information is shareable, whereas knowledge is one's property
(c) Information is stimulatory, whereas knowledge is practical
(d) None of these

7. 'Web of Science' is :
(a) A bibliographical index
(b) A critical index
(c) A citation index
(d) A bibliographical index

8. Transformation of traditional libraries to hybrid/ digital libraries is :
(a) Project management (b) Change management
(c) Survey management (d) Research management

9. Which one of the following is not a switching system?
(a) Packet (b) Messenger
(c) Massage (d) Router

10. Access to back volumes of e-journals is known as :
(a) Retrospective Access
(b) Random Access
(c) Perpetual Access
(d) Online Access

11. The Chi-square technique is used to compare the observed data with that of :
    (a) Analytical Data (b) Biological Data
    (c) Expected Data (d) Graphical Data
12. 'FRBR' is developed by :
    (a) IFLA (b) UNESCO
    (c) RRRLF (d) DRDO
13. Who were involved in Public Library Movement in India:
    (a) C.D. Deshmukh (b) S.R. Ranganathan
    (c) Both (a) and (b) (d) None of these
14. Which of the following are Library Network?
    (a) DELNET (b) INFLIBNET
    (c) OCLC (d) All of the above
15. Which of the following are review type services?
    (a) Trend Reports (b) State of the Art Report
    (c) Both (a) and (b) (d) None of these
16. The basic characteristics of a system are :
    (a) Arranged in hierarchical order
    (b) Interrelated components
    (c) Both (a) and (b)
    (d) None of these
17. The general image file format are :
    (a) JPEG (b) TIFF
    (c) PNG (d) All of the above
18. Which of the following are common types of protocols?
    (a) FTP (b) HTTP
    (c) Tednet (d) All of the above
19. Which of the following are not the elements of 'DOI' system?

(a) Subject (b) Description
(c) Policies (d) All of the above

20. Which of the following are trade bibliographies?
(a) Books in print (b) Indian Books in Print
(c) Both (a) and (b) (d) None of these

21. Where and when 'NICMAP' was established?
(a) Bangalore, 1977 (b) New Delhi, 1988
(c) Chennai, 1979 (d) Kolkata, 1980

22. The 'National Information Centre', New Delhi has been set up by?
(a) Delhi Library Association
(b) Higher Education Commission in India
(c) University Grant Commission in India
(d) Electronic Commission of India

23. Patent Information System, Nagpur is :
(a) Mission Oriented (b) Material Oriented
(c) Subject Oriented (d) Survey Oriented

24. An online Information System comes under the category of :
(a) Database Oriented (b) Database Producer
(c) Database Vendor (d) Database Product

25. The basic reference model of 'OSI' was issued in :
(a) 1977 (b) 1983
(c) 1979 (d) 1990

26. 'ITU' stands for :
(a) International Telecommunication Union
(b) Internal Telecommunication Union
(c) Internet Telecommunication Union
(d) Indian Telecommunication Union

27. Kernel Parts of UNIX directly interact with hardware?
    (a) True (b) False
    (c) Both (a) and (b) (d) None of these
28. Chain procedure, 'PRECIS' and 'POPSI' are the systems based on :
    (a) Numerical methods
    (b) Classificatory principles
    (c) Alphabetical methods
    (d) None of these
29. In 'KWIC' Indexes, the keyword appears :
    (a) At the beginning of each entry
    (b) At the centre of the line
    (c) At the end of the entry
    (d) None of these
30. Name the Vice-Chancellor who appointed him librarian of 'BHU'?
    (a) S. Radhakrishanan (b) S.R. Ranganathan
    (c) Dr. Zakir Hussain (d) Dr. Rajendra Prasad
31. The first commercial online information system is :
    (a) OCLC (b) DELNET
    (c) ORBIT (d) BLAISE
32. Focus on science and technology has increased because:
    (a) Knowledge commission has identified it as one of the potential area of development
    (b) US state department gives priority on S and T
    (c) World economy has become knowledge based
    (d) None of these
33. The following group of countries are the biggest investors in research :

(a) India, Britain, Japan, Koria
(b) France, Denmark, USA, U.K.
(c) China, Japan, France
(d) France, Japan, India

34. What is the cause of concern regarding foreign investment in research ?
(a) Sufficient methods of assess and evaluate the impact of such investment are not available
(b) Scientist and technicians involved in research are not paid well
(c) Both (a) and (b)
(d) None of these

35. Most foreign investment is being made in the area of :
(a) Grafting and Biography
(b) Grafting and Biology
(c) Computer Science and Automotive Design
(d) Physical Science and Planting

36. Foreign companies are outsourcing R and D programme to India because :
(a) Outsourcing is cost effective for foreign companies
(b) There is scarcity of skilled manpower in those countries
(c) Both (a) and (b)
(d) None of these

37. What is the main class number of "Political Science" according to 'DDC' classification method?
(a) 350 (b) 380
(c) 340 (d) 320

38. What is the main class number of "Economics" according to 'DDC' classification method?

(a) 330 (b) 310
(c) 350 (d) 370

39. What is the main class number of "Law" according to 'DDC' classification method?
(a) 320 (b) 330
(c) 340 (d) 350

40. What is the main class number of "Bible" according to 'DDC' classification method?
(a) 280 (b) 260
(c) 240 (d) 220

41. When 'INSDOC' was established?
(a) 1952 (b) 1956
(c) 1972 (d) 1976

42. Where is the headquarter of 'SENDOC'?
(a) Banglore (b) Pune
(c) Hyderabad (d) Kolkata

43 Under which organization 'DESIDOC' is functioning?
(a) ISOR (b) RRRLF
(c) CSIR (d) DRDO

44. What is user's profile?
(a) A list of user name list
(b) A list of user fill
(c) A list of users
(d) A statement of the Information Requirement of an user

45. What is matched with features of the documentation in SDI service?
(a) Document's profile (b) User's full name
(c) User's profile (d) None of these

46. E-books can be stored in :

(a) Hard disk server (b) DVD-ROMs
(c) CD-ROMs (d) All of the above

47. What are generally available e-documents?
(a) Internet (b) CD-ROMs
(c) Online Database (d) All of the above

48. Year books are also known as ?
(a) Annual (b) Weekly
(c) Yearly (d) Monthly

49. What is the base purpose of a yearbook?
(a) Record Annual Activities of a Subject
(b) Record Annual Activities of a Country
(c) Record Annual Activities of an Organisation
(d) All of the above

50. Which are Ready Reference sources in the following?
(a) Directories, Hand Book, Manuals
(b) Yearbook and Annuals
(c) Guides to Statistical Sources
(d) All of the above

51. What is a dictionary?
(a) Collection of data
(b) Collection of words
(c) Collection of knowledge
(d) User of words

52. When the second edition of Oxford English Dictionary was published?
(a) 1989 (b) 1870
(c) 1882 (d) 1980

53. Which type of Dictionary is just like an Encyclopedia?
(a) Special Dictionary (b) Technical Dictionary
(c) Subject Dictionary (d) Science Dictionary

54. What was the name of 'SUPER MARC' recommended by 'IFLA' working group in 1973?
    (a) UNIMARC (b) UK MARC
    (c) US MARC (d) MARC-21
55. The all current formats are originated from which format?
    (a) CCC (b) MARC
    (c) CCF (d) UNIMARC
56. "Biological Abstract" has four indexes i.e., Basic, Cross, Bio-systematic and :
    (a) Translator (b) Collaborator
    (c) Author (d) Publisher
57. "National Sample Survey Reports" comes under the category of which sources?
    (a) Primary (b) Secondary
    (c) Tertiary (d) None of these
58. In the classified parts of INB, the entries are arranged according to :
    (a) DDC 16th edition (b) UDC 5th edition
    (c) DDC 20th edition (d) CC 6th edition
59. "Africa Diary" is published :
    (a) Monthly (b) Yearly
    (c) Annually (d) Weekly
60. "World of Learning" is a :
    (a) Bibliography (b) Directory
    (c) Biography (d) Annual Reports

ANSWERS

1. (a)	2. (c)	3. (b)	4. (a)	5. (c)
6. (a)	7. (c)	8. (b)	9. (d)	10. (c)
11. (c)	12. (a)	13. (c)	14. (d)	15. (c)
16. (c)	17. (d)	18. (d)	19. (d)	20. (c)
21. (a)	22. (d)	23. (b)	24. (c)	25. (b)
26. (b)	27. (a)	28. (b)	29. (b)	30. (a)
31. (a)	32. (c)	33. (b)	34. (a)	35. (c)
36. (a)	37. (d)	38. (a)	39. (c)	40. (d)
41. (a)	42. (c)	43. (d)	44. (d)	45. (c)
46. (d)	47. (d)	48. (a)	49. (d)	50. (d)
51. (b)	52. (a)	53. (c)	54. (a)	55. (b)
56. (c)	57. (b)	58. (a)	59. (d)	60. (b)

Practice Set 16

1. The Tamil Nadu Public Libraries Act provider for library cess to be levied by :
   (a) Local Government only
   (b) Central Government
   (c) Central State Government
   (d) None of these
2. Pondicherry Public Library Act was passed in the year:
   (a) 1990 (b) 1995
   (c) 1993 (d) 1958
3. In which law of Library Science, Library Legislation is given emphasized?
   (a) First laws of library science
   (b) Second laws of library science
   (c) Thirst laws of library science
   (d) Fourth law of library science
4. The Basic Role of the library is to :
   (a) Collect only
   (b) Collect and preserve it
   (c) Collect and dissemination of information
   (d) None of these
5. 'ASLIB' was started in the year :
   (a) 1921 (b) 1924
   (c) 1926 (d) 1930
6. Reference catalogue of current literature was founded in 1874 by :

(a) Joseph Whitaker (b) H.P. Luhn
(c) Henry La Fountain (d) S.R. Ranganathan

7. Whitaker's cumulative book list is a publication of :
(a) Russia (b) New York
(c) China (d) Great Britain

8. 'ASLIB Book List' is an example of a :
(a) Classified Bibliography
(b) Current Bibliography
(c) Alphabetical Bibliography
(d) None of these

9. Who was the chairman of "National Policy on Library and Information System" (1986)?
(a) B.S. Kesavan (b) Kalpana Dasgupta
(c) D.P. Chattopadhyay (d) G. Bhattacharya

10. The significance of the year 2011 for LIS education in India is :
(a) Centenary Year
(b) Golden Jubilee Year
(c) Platinum Jubilee Year
(d) None of these

11. Digital reference service can be offered through :
(a) Fax (b) Ask your librarian
(c) OPAC (d) MARC

12. 'Biotechnology' is formed as a result of :
(a) Fission (b) Diffusion
(c) Fusion (d) None of these

13. The order of significance of "Thing, Material and Action" among various components of a compound subject was expanded by :
(a) E.J. Coates (b) Macforlane

(c) George R. Tarry (d) H.P. Luhn

14. Relation Database is :
    (a) A symbol Representing Relationship between two concepts
    (b) Manipulation command which relate records in different fillds
    (c) Both (a) and (b)
    (d) None of these

15. 'Sodhganga' is a repository of :
    (a) E-books (b) E-journals
    (c) E-dictionary (d) E-thesis

16. Which of the following tests can be employed for hypothesis testing?
    (a) Chi-square test (b) F-test
    (c) T-test (d) All of the above

17. RRRLF falls under the :
    (a) Ministry of Arts
    (b) Ministry of Culture
    (c) Ministry of Human Resource
    (d) Ministry of Education Department

18. 'Internet Public Library' is being maintained by :
    (a) Chicago University (b) University of London
    (c) Drexal University (d) University of Delhi

19. What are the major driving forces behind an 'Information Society'?
    (a) ICT (b) Internet
    (c) Both (a) and (b) (d) None of these

20. Which libraries are functioning as depository libraries?
    (a) Delhi Public Libraries
    (b) Connemora Public Libraries

(c) Both (a) and (b)

(d) None of these

21. Which of the following are "Inclusive Geographical Sources" :

(a) Dictionary (b) Map

(c) Atlas (d) Encyclopedia

22. Which principles are corollary to will picture principle?

(a) Cow-calf Principle (b) Whole-organ Principle

(c) Both (a) and (b) (d) None of these

23. The factors that influence computer file organization are :

(a) Speed of Access (b) Storage Space

(c) File Volatility (d) All of the above

24. Major problems of "Information Communication Technology" are :

(a) Information overlaod

(b) Information insecurity

(c) Both (a) and (b)

(d) None of these

25. Which of the following are "Open Source Content Management Systems"?

(a) Drupal (b) Joomla

(c) Open CMS (d) All of the above

26. What is the main class number of 'HISTORY' according to 'CC' (Colon Classification) Method?

(a) V (b) C

(c) D (d) F

27. What is the main class number of 'Literature' according to 'CC' (Colon Classification) Method?

(a) P (b) O

(c) R (d) S

28. What is the main class number of 'HUMANITIES AND SOCIAL SCIENCE' according to 'CC' (Colon Classification) Method?
    (a) P (b) OC
    (c) MZ (d) G
29. What is the main class number of 'EDUCATION' according to 'DDC' Method?
    (a) 330 (b) 350
    (c) 360 (d) 370
30. What is the main class number of 'SOCIOLOGY' according to 'CC' (Colon Classification) Method?
    (a) Y (b) C
    (c) D (d) O
31. What is the main class number of 'ZOOLOGY' according to 'DDC' Method?
    (a) 560 (b) 580
    (c) 590 (d) 460
32. 'Sear's List of Subject Heading' is mainly used in :
    (a) Small Libraries (b) National Library
    (c) University Library (d) Special Library
33. Whose name is related with the citation indexing?
    (a) H. P. Luhn (b) Melvil Dewey
    (c) S.R. Ranganathan (d) C.A. Cutter
34. According to 'CCC' which is not analytical entries:
    (a) Author Analytical (b) Title Analytical
    (c) Subject Analytical (d) Series Analytical
35. The classified catalogue is a :
    (a) Author Catalogue (b) Subject Catalogue
    (c) Title Catalogue (d) Dictionary Catalogue
36. Law of persimon emphasizes on :

(a) Saving the time (b) Saving of the money
(c) Over al economy (d) None of these

37. Which one is the 'Pseudo Name' in the following :
(a) Prem Chand
(b) Dinkar
(c) Fanishwer Nath Renu
(d) Mahadevi Verma

38. The name of the author of a book is not known, what we call the work :
(a) Analytic (b) Anonyms
(c) Antonyms (d) None of these

39. Which one is the last canon regarding cataloguing by Ranganathan :
(a) Canon of prepotence
(b) Canon of Cow-calf
(c) Canon of Recall Value
(d) All of the above

40. In which year the first edition of 'ALA Code' was published ?
(a) 1893 (b) 1890
(c) 1872 (d) 1910

41. Anglo American Code for cataloguing was first published in the year :
(a) 1908 (b) 1920
(c) 1921 (d) 1890

42. The title 'History of Library Science' is a case of :
(a) Phase relation (b) Common Isolate
(c) Science (d) Art

43. In CC (Colon Classification) P_2 represents :
(a) Second Level Personality

(b) First Level Personality
(c) First Level Protection
(d) None of these

44. Which one of the following does not give extrapolation:
(a) Title Device
(b) Subject Device
(c) Common Isolate Device
(d) Sector Device

45. In CC, the term like Classification, Documentation, Surgery, Radio Therapy denote :
(a) Energy Facet (b) Matter Facet
(c) Space Facet (d) Time Facet

46. What does 2P indicate in CC?
(a) First Personality
(b) First Round Personality
(c) Second Round Personality
(d) Second Personality

47. 'Mnemonics' means :
(a) Lose of memory (b) Aid to memory
(c) Fast memory (d) None of these

48. How many zones have been recognized by Ranganathan?
(a) 05 (b) 02
(c) 08 (d) 07

49. The classes belonging to same array are said to be :
(a) Classification (b) Coordinate
(c) Co-operation (d) Coordinated

50. In DDC 'Biographies and Genealogy' fall under which main class :

(a) 920 (b) 924
(c) 910 (d) 930

51. Which organization is the corporate author of DDC?
(a) UNESCO (b) IFLA
(c) FID (d) MEDLARS

52. In which year "International Classification" Scheme was first published?
(a) 1961 (b) 1960
(c) 1965 (d) 1957

53. The Index of DDC is called :
(a) Main Index (b) Relative Index
(c) Title Index (d) Subject Index

54. Who used category first in his classification scheme?
(a) C.A. Cutter (b) H.E. Bliss
(c) Melvil Dewey (d) S.R. Ranganathan

55. 'CC' is known as 'Colon Classification' because :
(a) Ranganathan's Liked Colon
(b) Colon was the symbol for energy
(c) Colon is the symbol of energy
(d) Colon was the only connecting symbol used when scheme was devised

56. On which item the most of the money of the budget of library is spent?
(a) Journals (b) Books
(c) Staff (d) Buildings

57. Funds for special libraries are provided from :
(a) Parental organization
(b) RRRLF
(c) Library Cess
(d) Library Fee

58. 'Zero Based Budget' means :
    (a) No increase in income
    (b) Budgeting a fresh
    (c) Both (a) and (b)
    (d) None of these
59. Annual report of a library is a:
    (a) Report of the past year
    (b) Report of the future year
    (c) Report of the Next year
    (d) Account of the year
60. What is the "Main Record of the Library"?
    (a) Stock Register
    (b) Accession Register
    (c) Main Catalogue Register
    (d) Subject Register

ANSWERS

1. (a)	2. (c)	3. (b)	4. (c)	5. (b)
6. (a)	7. (d)	8. (b)	9. (c)	10. (a)
11. (b)	12. (c)	13. (a)	14. (b)	15. (d)
16. (d)	17. (b)	18. (c)	19. (c)	20. (c)
21. (d)	22. (c)	23. (d)	24. (c)	25. (d)
26. (a)	27. (b)	28. (c)	29. (d)	30. (a)
31. (c)	32. (a)	33. (c)	34. (d)	35. (b)
36. (c)	37. (a)	38. (b)	39. (c)	40. (a)
41. (a)	42. (b)	43. (a)	44. (c)	45. (a)
46. (c)	47. (b)	48. (a)	49. (d)	50. (a)
51. (c)	52. (c)	53. (b)	54. (c)	55. (d)
56. (c)	57. (a)	58. (b)	59. (a)	60. (b)

Practice Set 17

1. When the word 'Information' was first used?
   (a) 1960 (b) 1955
   (c) 1951 (d) 1950
2. Who said that information is product and process both:
   (a) S.R. Ranganathan (b) Melvil Dewey
   (c) J. Martin (d) J. Smith
3. What is current contents :
   (a) Abstracting Service
   (b) Indexing Service
   (c) Translation Service
   (d) Current Awareness Service
4. 'AGRIS' was formerly known as :
   (a) Indexing Bulletin (b) Indexing Journal
   (c) Granthalaya (d) ILA Bulletin
5. Where is 'NASSDOC' Situated?
   (a) Pune (b) Mumbai
   (c) New Delhi (d) Kolkata
6. 'SENDOC' is meant for the documentation activities of :
   (a) Small enterprises (b) Information
   (c) Information product (d) Technology
7. Who inaugurated 'DRTC' of India in Bangalore :
   (a) S.R. Ranganathan (b) T. Viswanathan
   (c) B.S. Kesavan (d) G. Bhattacharya

8. Where is "Patent Information System" (PIS) situated ?
   (a) Kolkata (b) Ahmedabad
   (c) Pune (d) Nagpur
9. 'INIS' is example of :
   (a) Distribution input and output
   (b) Distributed input and centralized output
   (c) Both (a) and (b)
   (d) None of these
10. Who established 'IAEA' in 1957?
   (a) MEDLARS (b) UNO
   (c) UNESCO (d) IFLA
11. Who is the publisher of 'INIS atom index' :
   (a) UNESCO (b) NISSAT
   (c) DESIDOC (d) INIS
12. What is Research ?
   (a) A systematic method to obtain tentative solution of the problem
   (b) A method to obtain solution of the problem
   (c) Both (a) and (b)
   (d) None of these
13. Which type of computers, the 'PC' is :
   (a) Micro Computer (b) Super Computer
   (c) Mini Computer (d) Mainframe Computer
14. Which agency used Computer first in India ?
   (a) DELNET (b) National Library of India
   (c) ISI, Kolkata (d) RRRLF
15. When computer was applied first in India?
   (a) 1970 (b) 1956
   (c) 1957 (d) 1990

16. Research design give the :
    (a) Procedure of Research
    (b) Procedure for Design Tools
    (c) Blue Print of the Research Activity
    (d) None of these
17. What type of Research is the 'Chain Procedure' of Ranganathan?
    (a) Applied Research (b) Basic Research
    (c) Historical Research (d) Normetive Research
18. What is 'Basic Research'?
    (a) Fundamental of Research
    (b) Search for a Solution
    (c) Search for broad principles without objectives
    (d) None of these
19. What is the 'aim' of research?
    (a) To discover laws
    (b) To discover laws theories and principles
    (c) Both (a) and (b)
    (d) None of these
20. Which one of the following is the personalized service?
    (a) Translation Service
    (b) Current Awareness Service (CAS)
    (c) Reference Service
    (d) Select Dissemination of Information (SDI)
21. 'SDI' matches the document's profile with the :
    (a) User's Profile (b) Staff Profile
    (c) Book Profile (d) Author's Profile
22. In 'Colon Classification' (6th edition) 'LB' denotes :
    (a) Canon (b) Special
    (c) System (d) Rounds

23. According to S.R. Ranganathan the canons for chain are :
    (a) Canon of recall value
    (b) Canon of decreasing extension and modulation
    (c) Both (a) and (b)
    (d) None of these

24. When was the final 'ISBD' consolidation edition published by 'IFLA'?
    (a) 2011 (b) 2015
    (c) 2017 (d) 2016

25. 'Open Journal System' is an example of which of the following open access models?
    (a) Green (b) Vasa
    (c) Platinum (d) Gold

26. Identify the document which is published by H.W. Wilson?
    (a) Sears list of subject headings 20th edition, 2010
    (b) The Information who's who 78th edition, 2014
    (c) Europa World yearbook 55th edition, 2014
    (d) None of these

27. According to 'OCLC' research report know your communication and its needs is the rephrasing of which law of Ranganathan?
    (a) First law of library science
    (b) Second law of library science
    (c) Third law of library science
    (d) Fifth law of library science

28. Index Indiana, an index to Indian periodical literature is being compiled by :
    (a) Information library network, Ahmedabad
    (b) National information centre, Delhi

(c) Central reference library, Kolkata

(d) Delhi library network, Delhi

29. 'Time and Motion' study was enunciated by :

(a) Frank and William Gilberth

(b) Henry La Fountain

(c) Edward Evans

(d) George R. Tarry

30. What is RJ45?

(a) A node

(b) A network cable connector

(c) An electronic coupler

(d) None of these

31. 'SIP' the communication protocol for signaling and controlling multimedia communication stands for :

(a) Internet Session Protocol

(b) Session Initiation Protocol

(c) Sound Initiation protocol

(d) None of these

32. Which of the following is a measure of dispersion?

(a) Root mean square deviation

(b) Geometric mean

(c) Mode

(d) None of these

33. Which of the following Rights are granted for 'Literary Works' according to copyright law of India?

(a) To make translation

(b) To make any adaptation

(c) Both (a) and (b)

(d) None of these

34. Identify from the following the features of Tacit knowledge?
    (a) Cannot be Articulated
    (b) Resides in Human Mind
    (c) Both (a) and (b)
    (d) None of these
35. Which of the following are the examples of web-based learning and education?
    (a) Answer tipes (b) Moodle
    (c) Campys Bug (d) All of the above
36. Which of the following one two sections stated in 'IFLA Digital Reference Guidelines'?
    (a) The Administration of Digital Reference Service
    (b) The Practice of Digital Reference
    (c) Both (a) and (b)
    (d) None of these
37. Which of the following sites are offered by "Britannica Library" a product of Encyclopedia Britannica?
    (a) Children (b) Young Adult
    (c) Reference Centre (d) All of the above
38. Which of the following communication channels are used frequently in virtual reference service?
    (a) Instant messaging (b) Voice over I.P.
    (c) Both (a) and (b) (d) None of these
39. Identify the affinitive/associative relationship of the following ?
    (a) Genetic (b) Concurrent
    (c) Both (a) and (b) (d) None of these
40. Which of the following are the components of a master database in acquisition system/module?

(a) Vendor master (b) Currency master
(c) Both (a) and (b) (d) None of these

41. Which of the following are types of random samples?
(a) Cluster Sampling (b) Stratified Sampling
(c) Systematic Sampling(d) All of the above

42. Jubilee project is associated with what?
(a) Public Library Survey
(b) Evaluation of Electronic Information Service
(c) Information Library Centre
(d) Research Survey

43. The publisher of "Information Power Building partnership for Learning" is :
(a) American Library Association
(b) Indian Library Association
(c) UNESCO
(d) MEDLARS

44. In 1974 Zurkowski used for the first time which of the following term?
(a) Digital Literacy
(b) Communication Literacy
(c) Information Literacy
(d) None of these

45. Inference Engine is a part of which Information System?
(a) Expert System
(b) Management Information System
(c) Management by Objective
(d) Management System

46. Which of the following is not related case study approach in a research design?

(a) Study of limit case (b) General study

(c) Special Study (d) None of these

47. "Student visit to Library is influenced by the available of Internet" state "Students visit to Library" is which kind of variable?

(a) Independent variable

(b) Dependent variable

(c) Intervening variable

(d) None of these

48. Idiographic Hypothesis is directed towards predicting the behaviour of :

(a) Group of people (b) Massages

(c) An Individual (d) None of these

49. In the process of reasoning when we start with a specific statement, and conclude to a general statement, it is called :

(a) Inductive Reasoning (b) Deductive Reasoning

(c) Both (a) and (b) (d) None of these

50. Solomon four group design is related to :

(a) Information Analysis Model

(b) Pretest Post Test Control Group Design

(c) Knowledge Analysis Model

(d) All of the above

51. Internet filtering is :

(a) Acceptable user policy

(b) A form to censorship

(c) Both (a) and (b)

(d) None of these

52. Which one of the following is a bulletin board service on Internet?

(a) Yahoo (b) Search Enginer
(c) Picaso (d) Blog

53. 'Virus' is a software which can :
(a) Replicate itself (b) Manipulate data
(c) Damage computer (d) All of the above

54. Which one of the following protocol is used in file transfer over internet?
(a) FTP (b) FTTP
(c) HTTP (d) None of these

55. Scaler Chain Shows :
(a) A link in the chain
(b) Authority structure
(c) Chain for Locating Racks
(d) All of the above

56. Blair and moron evaluation study on retrieval effectiveness of full test search is called :
(a) STAIRS project (b) Cranefield projct
(c) Both (a) and (b) (d) None of these

57. In cataloguing the square brackets [ ] are used :
(a) To enclose statement of accompanying material
(b) To enclose information taken from outside
(c) Both (a) and (b)
(d) None of these

58. Which section of AACR-II (R) deals with serial publications?
(a) Part-A, Section 12 (b) Part-A, Section 10
(c) Part-A, Section 08 (d) Part-A, Section 15

59. When two or more basic subjects having same relational approach from a specific subject, the relation is termed as :

(a) Common isolate (b) Phase Relation
(c) Co-ordinate relation (d) Intra Array Relation

60. The concept of 'Stopword' list is relevant in the context of :
(a) Keyword Indexing (b) Chain Indexing
(c) Uniterm Indexing (d) Uniform Indexing

ANSWERS

1. (a)	2. (c)	3. (b)	4. (c)	5. (c)
6. (a)	7. (b)	8. (d)	9. (b)	10. (b)
11. (d)	12. (a)	13. (a)	14. (c)	15. (c)
16. (c)	17. (a)	18. (c)	19. (b)	20. (d)
21. (a)	22. (c)	23. (b)	24. (a)	25. (c)
26. (a)	27. (b)	28. (c)	29. (a)	30. (c)
31. (b)	32. (a)	33. (c)	34. (c)	35. (d)
36. (c)	37. (d)	38. (c)	39. (c)	40. (c)
41. (d)	42. (b)	43. (a)	44. (c)	45. (a)
46. (b)	47. (b)	48. (c)	49. (a)	50. (b)
51. (b)	52. (b)	53. (d)	54. (a)	55. (b)
56. (a)	57. (b)	58. (a)	59. (b)	60. (a)

Practice Set 18

1. A version of 'KWIC' augmented with author/name is called :
   (a) WADEX (b) KWOC
   (c) OPAC (d) KWAC
2. 'Segmentation' is associated with :
   (a) Reference service report
   (b) Library survey report
   (c) Market survey report
   (d) Indexing report
3. State of the art report generally highlights:
   (a) General Aspects (b) Technical Aspects
   (c) Special Aspects (d) All of the above
4. Who propounded 'minimum, middling and maximum theories; of reference service?
   (a) Samual Rothstein (b) Sayers
   (c) K.C. Ayyappa (d) D.W. Lewis
5. Even though 'xerography' is a photocopying method, but it is called :
   (a) Diazographic (b) Electrofax
   (c) Electrostatic (d) None of these
6. 'CODEN' is connected with :
   (a) Books (b) Index
   (c) Journals (d) Serials
7. Roget's International Thesaurus is a :
   (a) List of scientific terms

(b) Classified list of world
(c) List of standard terms
(d) None of these

8. Information about scale and projection can be found in :
(a) Geographical sources
(b) Historical sources
(c) Encyclopedia Britannica
(d) Directories

9. Who of the following is not the author of any reference book?
(a) Louis Shares (b) S.R. Ranganathan
(c) Maurice B Line (d) Mac Forlane

10. Identify the odd one out :
(a) ANSI (b) ESPN
(c) OPAC (d) CCC

11. Where is the headquarters of 'NIC'?
(a) Russia (b) USA
(c) Japan (d) New Delhi

12. Since when is the beginning of the "National Science Policy" (NSP) considered in India?
(a) 1950 (b) 1958
(c) 1960 (d) 1971

13. In which year did the government of India announce the new "National Education Policy"?
(a) 1970 (b) 1972
(c) 1986 (d) 1990

14. In collaboration with whom was the "National Technology Policy" formulated in India?
(a) DRDO (b) DRTC
(c) RRRF (d) CSIR

15. 'CSIR' stands for :
    (a) Council of Scientific and Industrial Research
    (b) Council of Science and Information Research
    (c) Council of Scientific and Information Research
    (d) Council of Science and Information Report
16. In which year did 'RRRLF' and 'ILA' submit a report to the Government of India to formulate a "National Library Policy"?
    (a) 1986 (b) 1972
    (c) 1984 (d) 1970
17. Where the first M.Phil. programme in Library and Information Science was started in India?
    (a) University of Punjab
    (b) University of Madras
    (c) University of Delhi
    (d) Banaras Hindu University (BHU)
18. Corollary for second law of Library Science is :
    (a) Free Books Service (b) Book for All
    (c) Journals for All (d) E-library Service
19. Which of the following is not the prerequisite for a 'National Information Policy'?
    (a) State Advisory Committee
    (b) Government Advisory Committee
    (c) Production of National Bibliography
    (d) None of these
20. World Intellectual Property Organisation is related to:
    (a) India (b) Canada
    (c) USA (d) United Nations
21. Redundancy of Information is :
    (a) Necessary and Always Desirable

(b) Unnecessary and should be eliminated
(c) Both (a) and (b)
(d) None of these

22. "The Fifth Discipline" is written by :
(a) Peter Senge (b) Peter Drucker
(c) Peter Martine (d) None of these

23. 'POSDCORB' is given by :
(a) Henry La Fountain (b) George R. Tarry
(c) Luther Gullick (d) S.R. Ranganathan

24. "Principle of Scientific Management" were given by :
(a) Peter Drucker (b) Melvil Dewey
(c) Henry Fayol (d) S.R.Ranganathan

25. Which of the following is 'ROM' memory?
(a) PROM (b) EEPROM
(c) Both (a) and (b) (d) None of these

26. Mouse can be used with :
(a) CDS (b) SOUL
(c) ISIS (d) CDS/ISIS

27. Magnetic Tape is :
(a) A Direct Access Device
(b) A Sequential Access Device
(c) Both (a) and (b)
(d) None of these

28. Library Software 'Suchika' is devised by :
(a) DESIDOC (b) INSDOC
(c) INFLIBNET (d) RRRLF

29. Window 'NT' come in :
(a) 3 versions (b) 4 versions
(c) 2 versions (d) 1 version

30. The term user interface originated in the late of :
    (a) 1980 (b) 1971
    (c) 1970 (d) 1976
31. A term "Bibliometrics" was first coined by ..... in .... Year?
    (a) Pritchard, 1969 (b) Ranganathan, 1939
    (c) Melvil Dewey, 1960 (d) Sayers, 1920
32. Which sources would you consult to know the "Impact Factor" of journal publications?
    (a) Web of Science (b) SCOPUS
    (c) Both (a) and (b) (d) None of these
33. Research is conducted to :
    (a) Generate new knowledge
    (b) Develop a Theory
    (c) Re-interpret existing knowledge
    (d) All of the above
34. Radio frequency Identification is used in Library for :
    (a) Circulation of Document
    (b) Classified Document
    (c) Cataloguing Documents
    (d) None of these
35. 'BIOS' Contain :
    (a) Bootstrap program
    (b) Convert character to code program
    (c) Both (a) and (b)
    (d) None of these
36. Science Citation Index is published by :
    (a) H.W. Wilson (b) Thomson Reuters
    (c) Melvil Dewey (d) S.R. Ranganathan

37. Where is the headquarters of 'UNISIST'?
    (a) New Delhi (b) New York
    (c) London (d) Paris
38. In which year was 'UNISIST' established?
    (a) 1971 (b) 1975
    (c) 1970 (d) 1980
39. Which Institute has a 'UNISIST' Cooperation scheme?
    (a) NAASA (b) DRDO
    (c) UNESCO (d) AGRIS
40. 'BSO' stands for :
    (a) Broad System of Organisation
    (b) Broad System of Ordering
    (c) Broad Scientific of Organisation
    (d) Broad System of Operational
41. In which year was the "Education and Training of Users to Scientific and Technical Information" published?
    (a) 1972 (b) 1980
    (c) 1990 (d) 1978
42. When was "Mizoram Public Library Act" Passed?
    (a) 1998 (b) 1990
    (c) 1993 (d) 1995
43. When was "Uttarakhand Public Library Act" Passed?
    (a) 2001 (b) 2005
    (c) 1999 (d) 1997
44. When was "lakshadweep Public Library Act" Passed?
    (a) 2007 (b) 2010
    (c) 2011 (d) 2008
45. When was "Manipur Public Library Act" Passed?

(a) 1995 (b) 1976
(c) 1971 (d) 1988

46. In which year was the "Bihar Library Association" established?
(a) 1933 (b) 1936
(c) 1924 (d) 1931

47. In which year was the "Punjab Library Association" established?
(a) 1929 (b) 1925
(c) 1936 (d) 1938

48. In which year was the "Delhi Library Association" established?
(a) 1932 (b) 1930
(c) 1939 (d) 1940

49. In which year "Association for Information Management" established?
(a) 1921 (b) 1924
(c) 1936 (d) 1941

50. How many teens, as per the Bic Survey, do not own a Pen?
(a) 100 (b) 200
(c) 300 (d) 400

51. What is the main concern of the Author?
(a) That the teens use computer
(b) That the teens use mobile phone
(c) That the teens have forgotten the art of hand writing
(d) None of these

52. Using the central point of the classroom communication as the beginning of a dynamic pattern of ideas is referred to as :

(a) Information mapping (b) Mind mapping
(c) Knowledge mapping (d) None of these

53. Aspects of the voice, other than the speech are known as :
(a) Para language (b) Personal language
(c) Physical language (d) All of these

54. Every type of communication is affected by its :
(a) Transmission (b) Verbal
(c) Numerical (d) Context

55. Attitudes, Actions and Appearances in the context of Classroom Communication are considered as :
(a) Impersonal (b) Verbal
(c) Non-verbal (d) None of these

56. Most often, the teacher-students communication is :
(a) Utilitarian (b) Ultra
(c) Critical (d) All of the above

57. Which association was founded by Dr. S.R. Ranganathan?
(a) Madras Library Association
(b) Bengal Library Association
(c) Bihar Library Association
(d) Gujarat Library Association

58. Who started first school in Librarianship in the world?
(a) C.A. Cutter (b) S.R. Ranganathan
(c) Melvil Dewey (d) H.E. Bliss

59. 'Milvil Dewey' related to which country?
(a) Canada (b) America
(c) Russia (d) England

60. "Dr. S.R. Ranganathan" related to which country?
(a) India (b) Japan
(c) Russia (d) America

ANSWERS

1. (a)	2. (c)	3. (b)	4. (a)	5. (c)
6. (d)	7. (b)	8. (a)	9. (c)	10. (b)
11. (d)	12. (b)	13. (c)	14. (d)	15. (a)
16. (c)	17. (c)	18. (b)	19. (c)	20. (d)
21. (b)	22. (a)	23. (c)	24. (c)	25. (c)
26. (b)	27. (c)	28. (a)	29. (c)	30. (c)
31. (a)	32. (c)	33. (d)	34. (a)	35. (a)
36. (b)	37. (d)	38. (a)	39. (c)	40. (b)
41. (a)	42. (c)	43. (b)	44. (a)	45. (d)
46. (b)	47. (a)	48. (c)	49. (b)	50. (a)
51. (c)	52. (b)	53. (a)	54. (d)	55. (c)
56. (a)	57. (a)	58. (c)	59. (b)	60. (a)

Practice Set 19

1. The basic elements of communication process are :
   (a) Source (b) Message
   (c) Both (a) and (b) (d) None of these
2. Documentation abstract started its publication in year:
   (a) 1969 (b) 1961
   (c) 1966 (d) 1956
3. The resource sharing strategy of a library may not include :
   (a) Personal Access (b) Restricted Access
   (c) Group Access (d) None of these
4. Who developed "Seven Faces of Information Literacy"?
   (a) Christine Susan Bruce
   (b) David Loerfscher
   (c) Lancaster
   (d) Henry La Fountain
5. In which year the term "Information Seeking" coined by T.D. Wilson?
   (a) 1961 (b) 1990
   (c) 1984 (d) 1981
6. "Indian Library Review" is a blog of :
   (a) Indian Library Association
   (b) National Library of India
   (c) Information Library Network
   (d) DRDO

7. "Information for All Programme" (IFAP) was launched by :
   (a) DRDO
   (b) DRTC
   (c) UNESCO
   (d) American Library Association (ALA)
8. AACR-2 is replaced by :
   (a) Library of congress subject headings
   (b) American Library Association
   (c) AACR-4
   (d) Resource Description and Access
9. D-base is :
   (a) System Software (b) Application Software
   (c) Historical Software (d) Internet Software
10. Berne Convention (1886) is concerned with :
   (a) Indexing (b) Bibliography
   (c) Copyright (d) Biography
11. The database Indian patents is published by :
   (a) UNESCO (b) NISCAIR
   (c) NASSDOC (d) RRRLF
12. Which one of the following is not a tool for 'Book Selection'?
   (a) Data India (b) Indian Books in Print
   (c) Books in Print (d) None of these
13. "National Book Trust" is an autonomous organization functioning now under the aegis of :
   (a) Ministry of Art and Cuture
   (b) Ministry of HRD
   (c) Ministry of Education
   (d) Ministry of Information and Broadcasting

14. Linux is an example :
    (a) Information Software
    (b) Tools Software
    (c) Application Software
    (d) System Software
15. Which of the following is not a section of a main entry in 'CCC' (Ed. 5) :
    (a) Leading Section (b) Name Section
    (c) Title Section (d) Tracing Section
16. "National Register of Translators" is maintained by :
    (a) UNESCO
    (b) Central Translation Mission
    (c) National Book Trust
    (d) National Translation Mission
17. "Contents by Journals" is an example of :
    (a) Current Awareness Service
    (b) Translation Service
    (c) Reference Service
    (d) Referral Service
18. Which of the following is a publication of "Central Reference Library", Kolkata?
    (a) Index Indiana (b) Library Journals
    (c) Library Bulletin (d) None of these
19. Critical Incident Technique primarily concentrates on:
    (a) Job Analysis
    (b) A Single Number
    (c) A Small Number of Individuals
    (d) None of these
20. Prolegomena is published in :

(a) 1931 (b) 1937
(c) 1933 (d) 1934

21. When was the 'Delivery of Book Act' passed in India?
(a) 1954 (b) 1960
(c) 1951 (d) 1956

22. Where is the "National Library of India"?
(a) New Delhi (b) Kolkata
(c) Patna (d) Ahemadabad

23. What is the main source of finance of public library :
(a) Student (b) Public
(c) Government (d) Users

24. To which word is the word Sayali associated in Sayali Ramamrit Ranganathan Associated?
(a) Mother (b) Father
(c) District (d) Village

25. The book "The measurement and evaluation of library services: is written by :
(a) Henry Fayol (b) F.W. Lancaster
(c) S.L. Baker (d) Both (b) and (c)

26. 'African Recorder' is which type of publication?
(a) Encyclopedia (b) Dictionary
(c) News Digest (d) Bibliography

27. Preparation of library budget without considering previous year budget is known as :
(a) Performance Budget
(b) Zero Based Budgeting
(c) Programme Budgeting
(d) All of the above

28. "Three Card System" was devised by :
(a) H.E. Bliss (b) C.A. Cutter

(c) Melvil Dewely (d) S.R. Ranganathan

29. Collection and serving are the activities of which section?
    (a) Budget Section (b) Maintenance Section
    (c) Acquisition Section (d) Circulation Section
30. The term 'Information Literacy' coined in :
    (a) 1970 (b) 1974
    (c) 1971 (d) 1980
31. How many National Libraries are in Italy?
    (a) 10 (b) 08
    (c) 05 (d) 11
32. Jack Mills (UK) recipient of the 'FID' Ranganathan Award for the year :
    (a) 1990 (b) 1980
    (c) 1984 (d) 1995
33. Opening data of British Museum to the public was :
    (a) 18th January, 1960 (b) 15th January, 1959
    (c) 21st January, 1965 (d) 18th September, 1860
34. 'H.E. Bliss' a great classificationist of the world, wrote a book of poem titled:
    (a) Better Late than Never
    (b) Literature of Book
    (c) Poems of Book
    (d) None of these
35. 'Penguinize' means in England :
    (a) Cataloguing Scheme
    (b) Published in a Pater Back
    (c) Classification Scheme
    (d) Serial publication

36. In which year of "Dr. S.R. Ranganathan" Born?
    (a) 25 August, 1892 (b) 16 August, 1892
    (c) 12 August, 1892 (d) 25 August, 1892
37. In which year of Five laws of Library Science book published?
    (a) 1931 (b) 1934
    (c) 1926 (d) 1933
38. What is the management principle rule of Henry Fayol?
    (a) Twelve (b) Seven
    (c) Fourteen (d) Eleven
39. In which year of 'Melvil Dewey' born?
    (a) 10 January, 1855 (b) 12 September, 1860
    (c) 15 August, 1863 (d) 10 December, 1851
40. In which year of 'C.A. Cutter' Born?
    (a) 14th March, 1837 (b) 12th February, 1836
    (c) 14th August, 1830 (d) 16th August, 1851
41. In which year of 'C.A. Cutter' died?
    (a) 6th September, 1903 (b) 8th October, 1903
    (c) 10th January, 1903 (d) 25th December, 1903
42. When Melvil Dewey Died?
    (a) 26th January, 1931 (b) 26th December, 1936
    (c) 26th September, 1931 (d) 26th March, 1931
43. Which level of management is responsible for execution of activities, supervision and monitoring?
    (a) Front level (b) Middle level
    (c) Top level (d) Lower level
44. Which one of the following is regarded as supplement to all types of Reference Sources?
    (a) Atlas (b) Dictionary

(c) Directories (d) Encyclopedia

45. Acquisition world of the document comprised of :
    (a) Selection of study materials
    (b) Book Selection
    (c) Selection, Procurement and Accessioning
    (d) None of these
46. Which scholar propounded 29 principle of management?
    (a) S.R. Ranganathan (b) George R. Tarry
    (c) C.A. Cutter (d) H.E. Bliss
47. Which scholar propounded '57' principles of management?
    (a) Kuntz (b) O Donal
    (c) Both (a) and (b) (d) None of these
48. Who is the 'Theory of Demand' book selection theory?
    (a) S.R. Ranganathan (b) Melvil Dewey
    (c) C.A. Cutter (d) H.E. Bliss
49. Who Introduced the 'Network Method in Book Exchange'?
    (a) British Museum Library
    (b) Library of Congress Library
    (c) London Library
    (d) Network Library
50. "Brown Charging and Discharging System" is the system of which country?
    (a) Russia (b) Canada
    (c) USA (d) India
51. What is the full form of 'P' out of 'POSDCORB'?
    (a) Paying (b) Planning
    (c) Post (d) POPSI

52. What is the full form of 'O' out of POSDCORB?
    (a) Organising (b) Operating
    (c) Organised (d) Organisation
53. What is the full form of 'S' out of POSDCORB?
    (a) Space (b) Staff
    (c) Staffing (d) Standards
54. What is the full form of 'D' out of POSDCORB?
    (a) Directory (b) Direction
    (c) Director (d) Directing
55. "Psychological Abstracts" was started in :
    (a) 1929 (b) 1927
    (c) 1926 (d) 1930
56. "Sociological Abstracts" is published how many time in a year:
    (a) 04 (b) 05
    (c) 06 (d) 10
57. "Indian Book Reporter" is a publication of :
    (a) Gujarat (b) Gurgaon
    (c) New Delhi (d) Kolkata
58. "Publisher Weekly" was started in the year :
    (a) 1876 (b) 1850
    (c) 1872 (d) 1848
59. The Heart of Computer is :
    (a) Mother Board (b) CPU
    (c) UPS (d) Input Device
60. A work station has :
    (a) 32-64 MB main memory
    (b) 8-16 MB main memory
    (c) 64-120 MB main memory
    (d) 120-160 MB main memory

ANSWERS

1. (c)	2. (c)	3. (b)	4. (a)	5. (d)
6. (b)	7. (c)	8. (d)	9. (b)	10. (c)
11. (b)	12. (a)	13. (b)	14. (d)	15. (b)
16. (d)	17. (a)	18. (a)	19. (c)	20. (b)
21. (a)	22. (b)	23. (c)	24. (d)	25. (d)
26. (c)	27. (b)	28. (d)	29. (b)	30. (b)
31. (b)	32. (c)	33. (b)	34. (a)	35. (b)
36. (c)	37. (a)	38. (c)	39. (d)	40. (a)
41. (a)	42. (b)	43. (b)	44. (d)	45. (c)
46. (b)	47. (c)	48. (a)	49. (d)	50. (c)
51. (b)	52. (a)	53. (c)	54. (d)	55. (b)
56. (b)	57. (b)	58. (c)	59. (b)	60. (a)

Practice Set 20

1. 'Parry Committee' was related to :
   (a) Public Library (b) National Library
   (c) Academic Library (d) University Library
2. None Bibliography Database contains :
   (a) Alphabetical Data (b) Statistical Data
   (c) Numerical Data (d) All of the above
3. Which is not the objective of an out reach service of a library?
   (a) Intended to attract new users
   (b) Intended to attracted regular users
   (c) Service Provided by a library outside its usual location
   (d) None of these
4. In which Indian state, there is no provision of library cess in its public library act :
   (a) Andhra Pradesh (b) Gujarat
   (c) Maharashtra (d) Tamil Nadu
5. What is the frequency of 'LISA'?
   (a) Monthly (b) Yearly
   (c) Weekly (d) Daily
6. Part 'J' of CCC (ed. 5) deals with :
   (a) Name of person (b) Name of publisher
   (c) Name of author (d) Rendering of Names
7. Stock verification is an activity of :
   (a) Accession Section (b) Maintenance Section
   (c) Cataloguing Section (d) Preservation Section

8. Process of moving up or down in a world processing documents is termed as :
   (a) Pull down (b) Scrolling
   (c) Both (a) and (b) (d) None of these
9. ASCII have how many codes?
   (a) 260 (b) 250
   (c) 256 (d) 290
10. Text book comes under the category of :
   (a) Secondary (b) Primary
   (c) Tertiary (d) None of these
11. Index Society of UK was founded in year :
   (a) 1851 (b) 1877
   (c) 1850 (d) 1860
12. Sear's list of Subject Heading was first published in :
   (a) 1931 (b) 1926
   (c) 1921 (d) 1923
13. Library of congress Subject Heading started published in the year :
   (a) 1915 (b) 1911
   (c) 1890 (d) 1896
14. Who defined notation as a shorthand sign?
   (a) E.C. Rechardson (b) S.R. Ranganathan
   (c) Melvil Dewey (d) W.B. Sayers
15. Division of labour is one of the principle of :
   (a) Administration
   (b) System Analysis
   (c) Management by objectives
   (d) Scientific management
16. 'Zero Base Budgeting' (ZBB) was developed by :

(a) Peter Phayor (b) Peter Drucker
(c) Henry Fayol (d) S.R. Ranganathan

17. Mac Calvin Principle of Book Section is also known as:
(a) Theory of Demand (b) Theory of Book Selection
(c) Selection of Demand (d) None of these

18. Parry Report comes in :
(a) 1960 (b) 1948
(c) 1950 (d) 1967

19. The United Serial and Book Exchange is situated in :
(a) New York (b) London
(c) Washington, D.C. (d) India

20. 'KARDEX' is used for receipt of :
(a) Journals (b) Periodicals
(c) Print Book (d) Directories

21. Ayyer Directory of Publication was started in the year:
(a) 1880 (b) 1860
(c) 1909 (d) 1890

22. Book Review Digest (BRD) was started in :
(a) 1910 (b) 1905
(c) 1921 (d) 1915

23. "Indian Book Reporter" is a publication of :
(a) Bangalore (b) Kolkata
(c) Gurugram (d) New Delhi

24. "University Handbook" is a publication of :
(a) AIU (b) INSDOC
(c) RRRLF (d) MEDLARS

25. "International Political Science Abstracts" is published from :

(a) Toranto (b) Chicago
(c) New York (d) London

26. Who is Bibliothecar?
(a) Librarian (b) Library Director
(c) Library Secretary (d) None of these

27. Date of Establishment of 'UNESCO' is?
(a) 15th August, 1960 (b) 10th August, 1945
(c) 4th November, 1946 (d) 11th September, 1945

28. What is the trade mark of Bantam Books, Inc. N.Y.?
(a) Hen (b) Dog
(c) Cock (d) Cow

29. "LIBRA" is a publication of :
(a) B.S. Kesavan (b) S.R. Ranganathan
(c) Melvil Dewey (d) University of Rajasthan

30. "Journal of Indexing and Reference Work" was started in the year :
(a) 1960 (b) 1966
(c) 1962 (d) 1952

31. Who was the first librarian to use the phrase 'Reference Interviews'?
(a) Melvil Dewey (b) Margret Hutchins
(c) C.A. Cutter (d) S.R. Ranganathan

32. "Facts on File" is a weekly digest of :
(a) Indian Event (b) World Event
(c) Asian Event (d) American Event

33. Who demonstrated the process of microphotography?
(a) C.A. Cutter (b) H.E. Bliss
(c) Benjamin Dancer (d) None of these

34. Which country does not publishes its own Bibliography?

(a) Canada (b) Africa
(c) UK (d) US

35. 'CAB' stands for :
(a) Commonwealth Agricultural Bureau
(b) Central Assembly Bureau
(c) Common Agricultural Bureau
(d) Common Atomic Board

36. Which of the following statement is correct :
(a) Reference Service
(b) CAS is one form of SDI
(c) SDI is one form of CAS
(d) None of these

37. In AACR-2, in case of sacred scriptures, the Heading part of the main entry is the :
(a) Uniform Tite (b) Translator
(c) Sub Title (d) Collective Titles

38. According to AACR-2, in Tracing Section of the Main Entry Card we record :
(a) Main Entry (b) Added Entry
(c) Title Entry (d) Author Entry

39. Colon (:) was first used in which classification scheme:
(a) Dewey Decimal Classification
(b) Subject Classification
(c) International Classification
(d) Colon Classification

40. The single idea that can go with any basic subject is called :
(a) Isolate (b) Common
(c) Space (d) Energy

41. What is most popular language of the computer :
(a) English Language (b) Machine Language
(c) Hindi Language (d) High Level Language

42. Result obtained in computers is called :
(a) Output (b) Input
(c) Hardware (d) Software

43. On which centre computer is field ?
(a) B (b) C
(c) D (d) A

44. Who is the fir emeritus professor in Library and Information Science in India ?
(a) B.K. Sharma (b) U.M. Thakur
(c) G. Bhattacharya (d) P.N. Kaula

45. Staff manual in the libraries is meant for :
(a) List of user
(b) List of Staff
(c) Guide to the Library Staff
(d) Staff Manual

46. When "Sadler Commission" was set up?
(a) 1917 (b) 1910
(c) 1921 (d) 1925

47. From which country 'Dickinson' come to India?
(a) Japan (b) Russia
(c) America (d) France

48. The 'diazo process' is extensively used for making copies of :
(a) Microfilme (b) Micro Document
(c) DVD Cassettes (d) CD-ROM

49. Logical Classification means division on :

(a) Science (b) Augic
(c) Logic (d) Phylosophy

50. What is 'National Plan'?
(a) To give some symbol for identity
(b) To give call number
(c) To give accession number
(d) To give class number

51. What is motivation?
(a) A psychological process
(b) A psycho-physiological process
(c) Both (a) and (b)
(d) None of these

52. Who did participate in AACR-1?
(a) ALA, LA, LC, CLA (Canadian Library Association)
(b) ILA, LA, ALA
(c) BLA, ILA, IFLA
(d) ALA, BLA, FILA

53. The title "History of Library Science" is a case of :
(a) History (b) Phase Relation
(c) Common Isolate (d) Science

54. In which year AACR-1 came out?
(a) 1961 (b) 1954
(c) 1966 (d) 1967

55. Information is the part of :
(a) Knowledge (b) Data
(c) Communication (d) Information Science

56. Which agency sponsors 'BONET'?
(a) CSIR (b) NISSAT
(c) INSDOC (d) NASSDOC

57. Who invented the 'Microchip'?
    (a) IBM (b) NASA
    (c) Intel (d) DRDO
58. Dr. S.R. Ranganathan's chain procedure is meant by ?
    (a) Driving Subject Headings
    (b) Cataloguing
    (c) Classification
    (d) Subject Index
59. What is Reference Service is the libraries?
    (a) Help of Staff
    (b) Help of the Readers
    (c) Help by Human Agency
    (d) None of these
60. Who is the co-editior of DDC (20th edition)?
    (a) Melvil Dewey (b) John P. Comaromi
    (c) W.C.B. Sayers (d) Foskett

ANSWERS

1. (a)	2. (c)	3. (b)	4. (c)	5. (a)
6. (d)	7. (b)	8. (b)	9. (c)	10. (a)
11. (b)	12. (d)	13. (b)	14. (a)	15. (d)
16. (a)	17. (c)	18. (d)	19. (c)	20. (b)
21. (a)	22. (b)	23. (c)	24. (a)	25. (d)
26. (a)	27. (c)	28. (c)	29. (d)	30. (b)
31. (b)	32. (b)	33. (c)	34. (d)	35. (a)
36. (c)	37. (a)	38. (b)	39. (d)	40. (a)
41. (b)	42. (a)	43. (b)	44. (d)	45. (c)
46. (a)	47. (c)	48. (b)	49. (c)	50. (a)
51. (a)	52. (a)	53. (c)	54. (d)	55. (a)
56. (b)	57. (c)	58. (a)	59. (c)	60. (b)

Practice Set 21

1. Symbols A-F are used in which one of the following ?
   (a) Colon Number System
   (b) Hexadecimal Number System
   (c) Decimal Number System
   (d) None of these
2. Which one of the following is not a search engine?
   (a) Google (b) Yahoo
   (c) Bing (d) Chrome
3. 'CSS' Stands for :
   (a) Collection Style Sheets
   (b) Compact Style Sheets
   (c) Cascading Style Sheets
   (d) None of these
4. 'MOOC' stands for :
   (a) Massive Open Online Course
   (b) Mass Open Online Course
   (c) Media Open Online Course
   (d) None of these
5. Binary equivalent of decimal number 35, is :
   (a) 1001110 (b) 1100110
   (c) 100001 (d) 100011
6. gif, jpg, bmp, png are used as extensions for files which store :
   (a) Image data (b) Video data
   (c) Audio data (d) Text data

7. Which of the Anthropogenic Activity Accounts for more than 2/3rd of global water consumption?
   (a) Industry (b) Hydropower generation
   (c) Agriculture (d) None of these
8. One of the Anthropogenic Sources of gaseous Pollutants Chloro Fluorocarbons (CFCs) in air is :
   (a) Foam Industry (b) Iron Industry
   (c) Plastic Industry (d) Pesticide Industry
9. In terms of Total CO_2 emissions from a country, identify the correct sequence :
   (a) China > USA > Russia > India
   (b) India > USA > China > Russia
   (c) USA > China > India > Russia
   (d) None of these
10. The cyclone 'Hudhud' hit the coast of which state?
   (a) Madhya Pradesh (b) Andhra Pradesh
   (c) Tamil Nadu (d) Mumbai
11. Which of the following is 'not' a Renewable Natural Resource?
   (a) Air (b) Water
   (c) Salt (d) Fresh Water
12. Which of the following are the Tools of Good Governance?
   (a) Social Audit (b) Citizen's Charter
   (c) Right to Information (d) All of the above
13. Which of the following powers, the president has in relation to Lok Sabha?
   (a) Summoning (b) Prorogation
   (c) Dissolution (d) All of the above
14. The interval between two sessions of parliament must not exceed :

(a) 6 months (b) 3 months

(c) 2 months (d) 9 months

15. Right to privacy as a Fundamental Right is implied in:
    (a) Right to Education
    (b) Right to Freedom
    (c) Right to Life and Personal Liberty
    (d) None of these
16. "Education is the manifestation of perfection already is man" was stated by :
    (a) Ravindra Nath Tagore
    (b) Radhakrishnan
    (c) Ramkrishan Paramhansh
    (d) Swami Vivekanand
17. Which of the following is not a prescribed level of teaching?
    (a) Reflective (b) Standing
    (c) Differentiation (d) None of these
18. Maximum participation of students during teaching is possible through:
    (a) Demonstration method
    (b) Lectured method
    (c) Derective method
    (d) None of these
19. Instructional aids are used by the teacher to :
    (a) Clearing concepts (b) Clarify the concepts
    (c) Effective Concepts (d) None of these
20. Attitude of the teacher that affects teaching pertains to :
    (a) Connective domain (b) Cognitive domain
    (c) Affective domain (d) All of the above

21. Where is 'DRTC' located?
    (a) Bangalore (b) Chennai
    (c) New Delhi (d) Kolkata
22. Where is the headquarter of 'DELNET'?
    (a) Kolkata (b) Goa
    (c) Delhi (d) Bangalore
23. When was the "National Medical Library of India" established?
    (a) June, 1950 (b) April, 1966
    (c) March, 1965 (d) July, 1960
24. When was the "Documentation Research and Training Centre" (DRTC) established?
    (a) January, 1960 (b) March, 1966
    (c) April, 1962 (d) February, 1968
25. When was the "Indian Association of Special Libraries and Information Centre" (IASLIC) established?
    (a) 3 September, 1955 (b) 20 August, 1960
    (c) 26 February, 1958 (d) 30 November, 1956
26. In which year was the first state library act passed for public library in India?
    (a) 1947 (b) 1939
    (c) 1956 (d) 1948
27. The library is the awakening power for the education of the mass community. Who said this?
    (a) Raja Ram Mohan Roy
    (b) Mahatma Gandhi
    (c) UNESCO
    (d) Ranganathan
28. One who has the practice of reading a book can be happy everywhere. Whose statement is this?

(a) Dr. Rajendra Prasad
(b) Mahatma Gandhi
(c) Dr. S.R. Ranganathan
(d) Dr. A.P.J. Abdul Kalam

29. Which libraries come in the special libraries?
(a) Research Library (b) Jail Library
(c) Department Library (d) All of the above

30. Which libraries come in the "Academic Library"?
(a) School Library (b) College Library
(c) University Library (d) All of the above

31. What is the first library of the country called?
(a) Special Library
(b) Public Library
(c) Central Public Library
(d) National Library

32. What is the name of the "National Library of France"?
(a) Bibliotheque National
(b) Church Library
(c) Bibliotheque Library
(d) None of these

33. What is the name of the "National Library of Russia"?
(a) British Library (b) Imperial Public Library
(c) The British Museum (d) None of the above

34. What is the "National Library of Russia" located?
(a) Penzza (b) UFA
(c) Samna (d) Moscow

35. In which year was Ranganathan's book Titled "Library Development Plan" published?
(a) 1939 (b) 1950
(c) 1947 (d) 1956

36. Where is the headquarters of the "Indian Library Association" at present?
   (a) Delhi (b) Ahemadabad
   (c) Chennai (d) Kolkata
37. What was the number of members of Indian Library Association till 2000Ad?
   (a) Around 8000 (b) Around 5000
   (c) Around 7000 (d) Around 3000
38. Where was the first conference of the "Indian Library Association (ILA)" and when was it held?
   (a) December, 1933 (b) September, 1933
   (c) January, 1933 (d) March, 1933
39. Which magazine was first started by the "Indian Library Association" in the year 1942?
   (a) Library Science (b) Library Science Journal
   (c) Library Journal (d) Library Bulletin
40. When did 'IASLIC' held its first "National Conference" and where?
   (a) 1960, Kolkata (b) 1955, Kolkata
   (c) 1956, New Delhi (d) 1961, Chennai
41. In which year was the publication "Vatican Code"?
   (a) 1931 (b) 1930
   (c) 1927 (d) 1926
42. What year did the last publication of 'CCC'?
   (a) 7th (b) 6th
   (c) 5th (d) 10th
43. Which organization developed and sponsored 'ISBD'?
   (a) ALA (b) UNESCO
   (c) ISBD (d) IFLA
44. Who developed "Chain Indexing"?

(a) C.A. Cutter (b) S.R. Ranganathan
(c) Melvil Dewey (d) G. Bhattacharya

45. How many paragraphs in the main entry according to the 'CCC'?
(a) Six (6) (b) Five (5)
(c) Three (3) (d) Four (4)

46. Who is the publisher of the "Sears List of Subject Headings"?
(a) Library of Congress
(b) American Library Association
(c) H.W. Wilson
(d) Melvil Dewey

47. In which year did the "Library of Congress" start the MARC-1 project?
(a) 1966 (b) 1964
(c) 1971 (d) 1963

48. What is the "Canon of Prepotency" related to?
(a) Classification (b) Reference Service
(c) Management (d) Cataloguing

49. How many regions are in AACR-2?
(a) 5 (b) 6
(c) 8 (d) 4

50. Who prepared the 'PRESIS'?
(a) G. Bhattacharya
(b) M.A. Gopinath
(c) Dr. S.R. Ranganathan
(d) Melvil Dewey

51. How many links are in the "Chain Procedure"?
(a) Two (b) Three
(c) Five (d) Six

52. In which year was "Patna University" established?
    (a) 1917 (b) 1914
    (c) 1911 (d) 1903
53. What the types of "Academic Libraries"?
    (a) Three (b) Two
    (c) Four (d) Five
54. What organization is a library?
    (a) Political (b) Religion
    (c) Social (d) None of these
55. In which year was the 'NISCAIR' established?
    (a) 1994 (b) 1991
    (c) 1999 (d) 2002
56. In which year was the "Library Advisory Committee" formed by the Government of India?
    (a) 1956 (b) 1961
    (c) 1959 (d) 1951
57. 'UGC' was established in which year?
    (a) 1956 (b) 1948
    (c) 1961 (d) 1967
58. Where is the headquarter of 'UGC'?
    (a) Chennai (b) Kolkata
    (c) New Delhi (d) Banglore
59. In which year did 'UGC' started the 'Book Bank Scheme'?
    (a) 1965-1966 (b) 1963-1964
    (c) 1970-1971 (d) 1969-1970
60. Since when is the introduction of the Network System in book charging and discharging system?
    (a) From 1900 AD (b) From 1850 AD
    (c) From 1800 AD (d) From 1947 AD

ANSWERS

1. (b)	2. (d)	3. (c)	4. (a)	5. (d)
6. (a)	7. (c)	8. (a)	9. (a)	10. (b)
11. (c)	12. (d)	13. (d)	14. (a)	15. (c)
16. (d)	17. (c)	18. (a)	19. (b)	20. (c)
21. (a)	22. (c)	23. (b)	24. (c)	25. (a)
26. (d)	27. (c)	28. (b)	29. (d)	30. (d)
31. (d)	32. (a)	33. (b)	34. (d)	35. (b)
36. (a)	37. (c)	38. (b)	39. (d)	40. (a)
41. (a)	42. (c)	43. (d)	44. (b)	45. (a)
46. (c)	47. (a)	48. (d)	49. (b)	50. (c)
51. (b)	52. (a)	53. (a)	54. (c)	55. (d)
56. (c)	57. (a)	58. (c)	59. (b)	60. (a)

Practice Set 22

1. Identify the Association that has changed its original name ?
   (a) SLA (b) SC
   (c) ALA (d) ILA
2. Conference proceedings are considered as …….. Documents?
   (a) Primary (b) Secondary
   (c) Territory (d) Conventional
3. Rules for dictionary catalogue were devised by :
   (a) S.R. Ranganathan (b) Melvil Dewey
   (c) C.A. Cutter (d) H.P. Luhn
4. RSS feed is a tool of :
   (a) Web 1.0 (b) Web 2.0
   (c) Web 3.0 (d) Web 4.0
5. An appropriate source to find out descriptive information is :
   (a) Gazetteer (b) Dictionary
   (c) Journals (d) Encyclopedia
6. Glossary is a :
   (a) List of technical words in knowledge
   (b) List of technical words in language
   (c) List of Technical words with definitions
   (d) List of technical words with information
7. One of the following search engine is exclusively meant for Scientific Information?

(a) SCIRUS (b) Google
(c) Yahoo (d) Search Engine

8. Technological gatekeeper is :
   (a) A process of transfer of technology
   (b) A process of transfer of information
   (c) An information mechanism of keeping user informed of relevant development
   (d) None of these

9. Who among the following honoured with "Nobel Prize" for his substantial contribution in :
   (a) S.R. Ranganathan (b) Henri La Fountain
   (c) H.P. Luhn (d) C.A. Cutter

10. The Farmington plan is associated with :
    (a) Library Co-operation
    (b) Library legislation
    (c) Library Classification
    (d) Library Service

11. 'UNESCO' assisted model public library in India is located at :
    (a) Mumbai (b) Ahemadabad
    (c) Chennai (d) Delhi

12. Mark the odd one out :
    (a) Principle of Osmosis (b) Cow-calf principle
    (c) Both (a) and (b) (d) None of these

13. Shelf list facilitates :
    (a) Cataloguing (b) Stock Verification
    (c) Preservation (d) Cataloguing

14. 'GUI' stands for :
    (a) Grant University in India

(b) Great Unique Information
(c) Graphic User Interface
(d) None of these

15. The office of patent information system in India is at :
(a) Nagpur (b) Patna
(c) Ahemadabad (d) Chennai

16. Questionnaire is a :
(a) Tool for knowledge collection
(b) Tool for data collection
(c) Data Analysis Tool
(d) None of these

17. A periodical evaluation of an employee is done through :
(a) Data management
(b) Job analysis
(c) Performance appraisal
(d) None of these

18. 'Controlled Group' is a term used in :
(a) Research methodology
(b) Experimental Research
(c) Research Tool
(d) Historical Research

19. 'Noise' in Information Retrieval is due to :
(a) Recall Value (b) Cow-calf
(c) Precision (d) None of these

20. The concept "Invisible College" first used by :
(a) Derek Solla Price (b) Eugene Garfield
(c) Both (a) and (b) (d) None of these

21. Who enunciated the term "hypertext"?

(a) Ted Nelson (b) Bill Gates
(c) William (d) None of these

22. What are the 3 level of management?
(a) Only middle level
(b) Middle, Top and Operational
(c) Only Top Level
(d) None of these

23. Who was the chairman of National Library Committee:
(a) B.S. Jha (b) P.N. Kaula
(c) K.P. Sinha (d) B.S. Keshwan

24. The national library of India receives books under :
(a) The Copyright Act, 1985
(b) Delivery of Books Act, 1956
(c) Delivery of Books Act, 1954
(d) None of these

25. What is the past name of National Library of India?
(a) Culcutta Public Library
(b) Indian Library
(c) Kolkata Library
(d) Imperial Library

26. A system contains :
(a) Inter Related Parts having a purpose
(b) Intra Faceted
(c) Collected Parts
(d) None of these

27. In which year Hunter Commission was appointed :
(a) 1882 (b) 1860
(c) 1850 (d) 1870

28. Hunter Commission emphasized on which of the following :

(a) Establishment of University
(b) Establishment of School and College Libraries
(c) Establishment of College
(d) None of these

29. What is the main class number of 'BOTANY' according to 'CC' method?
(a) C (b) K
(c) P (d) I

30. What is the main class number of 'AGRICULTURE' according to 'CC' method?
(a) J (b) D
(c) E (d) B

31. What is the main class number of 'TECHNOLOGY' according to 'CC' method?
(a) E (b) F
(c) C (d) P

32. What is the main class number of 'LAW' according to 'CC' method?
(a) R (b) Q
(c) Z (d) S

33. What is the main class number of 'FINE ARTS' according to 'CC' method?
(a) N (b) O
(c) S (d) T

34. What is the main class number of 'PHILOSOPHY' according to 'DDC' method?
(A) 400 (B) 350
(C) 200 (D) 100

35. What is the main class number of 'LITERATURE' according to 'DDC' method?

(a) 600 (b) 300
(c) 800 (d) 900

36. What is the main class number of 'WOMEN EDUCATION' according to 'DDC' method?
(a) 350 (b) 376
(c) 380 (d) 385

37. What is the main class number of 'TEACHING' according to 'DDC' method?
(a) 385 (b) 370
(c) 371 (d) 400

38. What is the main class number of 'ASTRONOMY' according to 'DDC' method?
(a) 550 (b) 560
(c) 540 (d) 520

39. What is the main class number of 'BIOGRAPHY' according to 'Expensive Classification Scheme'?
(a) F (b) E
(c) C (d) G

40. What is the main class number of 'FICTION' according to 'Expensive Classification Scheme'?
(a) V6 (b) X
(c) T (d) X6

41. What is the main class number of 'SOCIAL SCIENCE' according to 'Expensive Classification Scheme'?
(a) F (b) S
(c) H (d) C

42. What is the main class number of 'MUSIC' according to 'Library of Congress Classification Scheme'?
(a) C (b) M
(c) D (d) T

43. 'Cornfield Project' is an example of :
    (a) Case Study (b) Library Management
    (c) Weeding (d) Research Report
44. IFLA took up the "Universal Availability of Publication" program in the year:
    (a) 1976 (b) 1950
    (c) 1970 (d) 1995
45. International Information System on Research in Documentation (ISORID) was:
    (a) INFLIB (b) AGRIS
    (c) UNESCO (d) DRDO
46. What is the relationship between ISBD and Cataloguing Code?
    (a) Cataloguing codes will include bibliographic description
    (b) Classification schemes
    (c) Cataloguing code will include biographical
    (d) None of these
47. COPSAT stands for :
    (a) Current Operational Patent in Science and Technology
    (b) Current Online Patent in Science and Technology
    (c) Co-operation Patent in Science and Technology
    (d) None of these
48. The Journal "Knowledge Organization" is published by :
    (a) DRDO (b) ISRO
    (c) ISKO (d) FID
49. Tagging in web 2.0 application is called :
    (a) Syndication (b) Synopsis
    (c) Directories (d) Encyclopedia

50. The Ranganathan Committee for University and College Libraries in India was constituted by :
   (a) Raja Ram Mohan Roy Library Foundation
   (b) University Grant Commission
   (c) Ministry of Planning Commission
   (d) None of these

51. In which year was the "Poona Library Network" (PUNENET) established :
   (a) 1992 (b) 1984
   (c) 1998 (d) 1995

52. In which year was the "Ahamadabad Library Network" (ADINET) established?
   (a) 1980 (b) 1983
   (c) 1999 (d) 1993

53. In which year was the "Management Library Network" (MANLIBNET) established?
   (a) 1998 (b) 2001
   (c) 2000 (d) 2010

54. In which year was the "Baroda State Library Association" established?
   (a) 1920 (b) 1926
   (c) 1936 (d) 1948

55. Software refer to :
   (a) Computer Instructions or Program that tell the hardware what to do
   (b) Any part of the computer that you can see
   (c) Both (a) and (b)
   (d) None of these

56. Empirically verifiable observation is :
   (a) Observational (b) Management Skills
   (c) Theory (d) Fact

57. The society for information science (SIS) was formed in :
    (a) 1960 (b) 1967
    (c) 1975 (d) 1980
58. Cannon of "Mixed Notation" is a cannon of :
    (a) Knowledge Plan (b) Verbal Plan
    (c) Informed Plan (d) Notational Plan
59. What type of species of classification of 'DDC' is :
    (a) Faceted (b) Enumerative
    (c) All most Normative (d) None of these
60. Who sponsors "NASSDOC" :
    (a) DRDO (b) ICSSR
    (c) UNESCO (d) MEDLARS

ANSWERS

1. (a)	2. (a)	3. (c)	4. (b)	5. (d)
6. (c)	7. (a)	8. (c)	9. (b)	10. (a)
11. (d)	12. (a)	13. (b)	14. (c)	15. (a)
16. (b)	17. (c)	18. (b)	19. (c)	20. (b)
21. (a)	22. (b)	23. (a)	24. (c)	25. (d)
26. (a)	27. (a)	28. (b)	29. (d)	30. (a)
31. (b)	32. (c)	33. (a)	34. (d)	35. (c)
36. (b)	37. (c)	38. (d)	39. (b)	40. (a)
41. (c)	42. (b)	43. (a)	44. (c)	45. (c)
46. (a)	47. (b)	48. (c)	49. (a)	50. (b)
51. (a)	52. (d)	53. (c)	54. (b)	55. (a)
56. (d)	57. (c)	58. (d)	59. (b)	60. (b)

Practice Set 23

1. What type of materials can be made available in microforms?
   (a) Out of print materials
   (b) Back files of newspapers
   (c) Both (a) and (b)
   (d) None of these
2. Inductive logic proceeds from :
   (a) Particular to general
   (b) General to personal
   (c) Particular to personal
   (d) None of these
3. Which of the following is not a "Graphic Representation"?
   (a) ISBN (b) Pin Code
   (c) Bar Chart (d) Index
4. "Fair Use" is a term most relevant to :
   (a) Reference book (b) Copyright
   (c) Management tool (d) None of these
5. Which of the following is not covered under Intellectual Property Rights?
   (a) Thesaurus (b) Patents
   (c) Dictionaries (d) Encyclopedias
6. Ontology is :
   (a) Long Range Reference Services
   (b) Indexing and Abstracting

(c) Reference Service in Library
(d) Classification of Internet Based Documents

7. Mozilla is :
(a) A Computer Software
(b) A Web Browser
(c) A Library Software
(d) None of these

8. Principles of Management are identified by :
(a) Peter Drucker (b) S.R. Ranganathan
(c) Henry Fayol (d) C.A. Cutter

9. Management by Objective (MBO) introduced by :
(a) Peter Drucker (b) S.R. Ranganathan
(c) Melvil Dewey (d) Sayers

10. 'POSDCORB' is coined by :
(a) C.A. Cutter (b) B.S. Keshwan
(c) H.E. Bliss (d) Luther Gullick

11. Who is the father of scientific management?
(a) Henry Fayol (b) F.W. Taylor
(c) Peter Drucker (d) B.S. Keshavan

12. The number of principles given by Fayol are :
(a) Seven (b) Nine
(c) Fourteen (d) Fifty Nine

13. Who gave the "Theory of Demand" for Book Selection?
(a) Dury (b) Drucker
(c) Gullick (d) Ranganathan

14. Who is known as father of Management?
(a) Luther Gullick (b) Henery Fayol
(c) S.R. Ranganathan (d) C.A. Cutter

15. "Fumigation" the term is related with :

(a) Circulation (b) Classification

(c) Conservation (d) Preservation

16. Who gave the basic principle of Book Selection in 1930?

(a) Dury (b) Ranganathan

(c) Cutter (d) Dewey

17. Who introduced 'Network' charging and discharging:

(a) The British Library

(b) London State Library

(c) Newark State Library

(d) New York Central Library

18. Who gave the principle of work division?

(a) Library Management

(b) Scientific Management

(c) Classification

(d) None of these

19. Unity of work, unity of direction and expansion of control is principle of :

(a) Circulation (b) Cataloguing

(c) Classification (d) Management

20. Brown charging and discharging system belong to :

(a) India (b) USA

(c) Britain (d) Japan

21. Three card system of periodical management was introduced by whom?

(a) S.R. Ranganathan (b) C.A. Cutter

(c) Melvil Dewey (d) H.E. Bliss

22. Who gave the demand and supply theory of books?

(a) Sayers (b) Mc Calvin

(c) Peter Drucker (d) P.N. Kaula

23. "To provide the best books to the maximum readers at the least cost" said by :
    (a) S.R. Ranganathan (b) Melvil Dewey
    (c) Assadullah (d) None of these
24. Theory of 'X' and Theory of 'Y' is developed by :
    (a) Douglas Mc Gregor (b) Mc Calvin
    (c) Peter Drucker (d) Melvil Dewey
25. ISBN now consists how many digits:
    (a) 16 (b) 12
    (c) 11 (d) 13
26. ISSN now consists how many digits?
    (a) 18 (b) 15
    (c) 10 (d) 13
27. Herzberg's Theory deals with :
    (a) Management (b) Classification
    (c) Preservation (d) Motivation
28. Critical Path Method (CPM) is developed by :
    (a) Ranganathan Company
    (b) Dupoint Company
    (c) Sharda Ranganathan Press
    (d) IFLA
29. Main use of shelf list is :
    (a) Management (b) Circulation
    (c) Stock Verification (d) Preservation
30. Which National Agency in India is Responsible for assigning the ISBN?
    (a) University Grant Commission
    (b) Raja Ram Mohan Roy Library Foundation
    (c) National Informatic Centre
    (d) National Library of India

31. In which year was term "Information Science" first used?
    (a) 1959 (b) 1970
    (c) 1955 (d) 1948

32. In which year was the first term for "Information"?
    (a) 1962 (b) 1955
    (c) 1970 (d) 1960

33. In which year was the "patent" bill passed in India?
    (a) 1956 (b) 1955
    (c) 1970 (d) 1972

34. In which year was the "Copy Right Act" passed in India?
    (a) 1900 (b) 1847
    (c) 1850 (d) 1890

35. In which year was the "Scientific Policy" passed in India?
    (a) 1970 (b) 1948
    (c) 1955 (d) 1958

36. In which year was Ranganathan's "Five Law of Library Science" published?
    (a) 1931 (b) 1933
    (c) 1934. (d) 1928

37. Since when is the beginning of the library movement in India considered?
    (a) 1936 (b) 1947
    (c) 1911 (d) 1921

38. In which year was the "Library Act" passed in England?
    (a) 1800 (b) 1850
    (c) 1903 (d) 1890

39. In which year was the "Library Act" passed in Russia?
    (a) 1921 (b) 1868
    (c) 1872 (d) 1900
40. In which year was "Kolkata University Commission" formed?
    (a) 1921 (b) 1911
    (c) 1910 (d) 1917
41. Who was nominated the first chairman of "Kolkata University Commission"?
    (a) B. Murti (b) M. Sandler
    (c) John Carry (d) B.S. Keshwan
42. Under whose chairmanship was the formation of the "University Grant Commission" in India?
    (a) C.D. Deshmukh (b) S.R. Ranganathan
    (c) B.S. Keshwan (d) None of these
43. In which year was the "University Education Commission" formed in India?
    (a) 1956 (b) 1948
    (c) 1954 (d) 1947
44. The University Education Commission in India was formed under whose chairmanship?
    (a) C.D. Deshmukh (b) S.R. Ranganathan
    (c) Radha Krishnan (d) W. Bordan
45. In which year was the first "All India Library Association" established in India?
    (a) 1933 (b) 1948
    (c) 1928 (d) 1942
46. Who is the founder of "Indian Library Assocation"?
    (a) C.D. Deshmukh (b) S.R. Ranganathan
    (c) M. Shadlar (d) Radhakrishnan

47. In which year was the "American Library Association" established?
    (a) 1800 (b) 1850
    (c) 1860 (d) 1876
48. In which year was the "IASLIC" established?
    (a) 1972 (b) 1948
    (c) 1955 (d) 1976
49. Where was 'IASLIC' established in India?
    (a) Ahamedabad (b) Delhi
    (c) Mumbai (d) Kolkata
50. Where was 'FID' established?
    (a) The Hague (b) London
    (c) Russia (d) India
51. What may be called to the databases of telephone directory, railway time table directory etc.?
    (a) Subjective Database (b) Alphabetical Database
    (c) Numerical Database (d) Alphanumeric Database
52. When the term "Quality Management" was first started to use in western countries?
    (a) 1975 (b) 1940
    (c) 1980 (d) 1960
53. In which year "Yahoo" search engine was launched?
    (a) 1994 (b) 2000
    (c) 2005 (d) 2001
54. Why the Hypothesis is generalized?
    (a) For writing (b) For practical use
    (c) For Numeric (d) For Search
55. Zero Based Budgeting System was propounded by :
    (a) Peter Drucker (b) Peter Phyrr
    (c) S.R. Ranganathan (d) Mc Calvin

56. When "Zero Based Budgeting System" was first :
   (a) 1985 (b) 1965
   (c) 1955 (d) 1970
57. Posting the Right Person at the Right Place is called:
   (a) Circulation (b) Recruitment
   (c) Development (d) System
58. TQM is a system of continuous improvement employing participative management and centered on needs of the :
   (a) Organisation (b) Budgeting
   (c) Staffing (d) None of these
59. Budget which mainly covers item of current revenues and expenditure is called :
   (a) Current Budget (b) Programme
   (c) Capital Budgeting (d) Zero Based Budgeting
60. What are the two parts of the Annual Report of the Library?
   (a) Statistical
   (b) Descriptive and Statistical
   (c) Primary
   (d) Secondary

ANSWERS

1. (c)	2. (a)	3. (c)	4. (b)	5. (a)
6. (d)	7. (b)	8. (c)	9. (a)	10. (d)
11. (b)	12. (c)	13. (a)	14. (b)	15. (d)
16. (a)	17. (c)	18. (b)	19. (d)	20. (b)
21. (a)	22. (b)	23. (b)	24. (a)	25. (d)
26. (b)	27. (d)	28. (b)	29. (c)	30. (b)
31. (a)	32. (d)	33. (c)	34. (b)	35. (d)
36. (a)	37. (c)	38. (b)	39. (a)	40. (d)
41. (b)	42. (a)	43. (b)	44. (c)	45. (a)
46. (b)	47. (d)	48. (c)	49. (d)	50. (a)
51. (d)	52. (c)	53. (a)	54. (b)	55. (b)
56. (d)	57. (b)	58. (a)	59. (c)	60. (b)

Practice Set 24

1. The concept of concretes and processes was given by :
   (a) C.A. Cutter (b) P.N. Kaula
   (c) S.R. Ranganathan (d) B.S. Keshwan
2. Chairman of National Knowledge Commission is :
   (a) Sam Pitroda (b) Dr. Manmohan Singh
   (c) Rajnath Singh (d) Narendra Modi
3. High Level language is :
   (a) C (b) Machine Independent
   (c) C+ (d) Java
4. The transmission of Receiver's reaction back to the sender is known as :
   (a) Circulation (b) Management
   (c) Source (d) Feedback
5. Currently "Science Citation Index" is published by :
   (a) Ess Ess Publication (b) Thomson
   (c) Janki (d) Oxford
6. Protocol means :
   (a) Interchange of data between two computers
   (b) Interchange of data between two device
   (c) Both (a) and (b)
   (d) None of these
7. Who is the Pioneer of "Open Access System" in British Library?
   (a) C.A. Cutter (b) J.D. Brown
   (c) Neena Brown (d) Mc Calvin

8. What is "J.D. Brown's" full Name?
   (a) James Day Brown (b) James Duff Brown
   (c) James Dot Brown (d) Jimmy Duff Brown
9. When was New York charging system started?
   (a) 1920 (b) 1850
   (c) 1800 (d) 1900
10. Who started New York charging system?
   (a) John Carry (b) John Cotton Dana
   (c) C.A. Cutter (d) Melvil Dewey
11. How many columns are there in the Accession Register?
   (a) 14 (b) 10
   (c) 11 (d) 16
12. When was 'PERT' developed?
   (a) 1970 (b) 1948
   (c) 1958 (d) 1947
13. Intra Facet Phase Relation is used for representing relationship between :
   (a) Two Isolates belonging to the same facet
   (b) Two Isolates belonging to the different subject
   (c) Two Isolates belonging to the same subject
   (d) None of these
14. In 'UDC' common isolates are called :
   (a) Subject Division (b) Common Auxiliaries
   (c) Form Division (d) Common Command
15. "University Handbook" is published by :
   (a) Information Library Network
   (b) University Grant Commission
   (c) Association of Indian Universities
   (d) National Informatic Centre

16. Who developed the "Dynamic Theory of Classification"?
    (a) Ranganathan and his associates
    (b) Melvil Dewey
    (c) C.A. Cutter and his associates
    (d) Browne and his associates
17. Cannon of exhaustiveness is one of the cannon of :
    (a) Chain (b) Isolate
    (c) Array (d) Notation
18. In 'CC' the main class C-Physics is further divided in to :
    (a) Generic Class (b) Canonical Class
    (c) Compound Class (d) None of these
19. In cataloguing the square brackets [ ] are used for :
    (a) To enclose information taken from outside
    (b) To enclose the statement of accompanying material
    (c) Both (a) and (b)
    (d) None of these
20. Who was the chairman of UGC committee on National Network System for universities libraries?
    (a) S.R. Ranganathan (b) B.S. Keshwan
    (c) P.N. Kaula (d) Yash Pal
21. "Information Science Abstract" developed by :
    (a) Library Journal Press
    (b) Documentation Abstract
    (c) Library Abstract
    (d) Technology Abstract
22. Large Group Communication generally involves :
    (a) 27 persons (b) 20 persons
    (c) 17 persons (d) 31 persons

23. Institute of Librarians was formed in year :
    (a) 1988 (b) 1995
    (c) 1960 (d) 1975
24. "Every Book Its Reader" is :
    (a) First law of library science
    (b) Third law of library science
    (c) Fifth law of library science
    (d) Fourth law of library science
25. Right book to the right reader in right time is according to :
    (a) Drucker (b) Cutter
    (c) Dury (d) Dewey
26. Modern Librarian Periodical started by Punjab University Association in the year :
    (a) 1930 (b) 1932
    (c) 1925 (d) 1941
27. Public Library manifesto published by 'UNESCO' first in :
    (a) 1957 (b) 1960
    (c) 1949 (d) 1947
28. International Standard Book Description does not standardize :
    (a) Type of information to be included in the catalogue entry
    (b) The points of access
    (c) Both (a) and (b)
    (d) None of these
29. 'JOCLAI' includes :
    (a) American Library Association
    (b) Indian Library Association

(c) The National and State Library Association

(d) None of these

30. According to 'CCC' ministry of finance is an example of :

(a) Executive body (b) Legislator body

(c) Government body (d) None of these

31. 'ZOTERO' is a :

(a) Bibliographic Reference Management System

(b) Management System

(c) Library Circulation Method

(d) Cannon of Classification

32. "MENDELEY" is developed by :

(a) S.R. Ranganathan (b) C.A. Cutter

(c) Elsevier (d) Melvil Dewey

33. "URKUND" offers :

(a) Library Management Tools

(b) Detect and Prevent Plagiarism

(c) Online Catalogue Card

(d) None of these

34. "Research in Progress" database in India is :

(a) Shodhganga (b) Shodhgangotri

(c) Shakti Vidyapith (d) National Library of India

35. The person who prepares Dictionary is known as :

(a) Biographer (b) Bibliographer

(c) Classifier (d) Lexicographer

36. Which of the following is an "Acronym"?

(a) ALA (b) UNESCO

(c) AGRIS (d) MEDLARS

37. A set of rules that govern overall data communication system is popularly known as :

(a) Database (b) Agreement
(c) Analytical (d) Protocol

38. Staffing is concerned with providing and maintaining resources :
(a) Analysis (b) Human
(c) Budget (d) Technology

39. What is the meaning of "Translation Pools"?
(a) Agency of the names of Translation Experts
(b) Agency of the Names of Transmission Tools
(c) Details about the Names of Translation Experts
(d) None of the above

40. How is Stochastic equation of information solved?
(a) By Chronological Rules
(b) By Statistical Rules
(c) By Dynamic Rules
(d) None of these

41. Who is awarded first 'Ph.D.' in Library Science from an Indian University?
(a) D.B. Krishna Rao (b) S.R. Ranganathan
(c) P.N. Kaula (d) Assadullah

42. How many phase relations are there in CC-7 edition?
(a) Eight (b) Four
(c) Six (d) Five

43. How many Total Notational Symbols are there in CC-7 edition?
(a) 25 (b) 11
(c) 18 (d) 14

44. Journal of Information Processing is published by :
(a) Information Processing Society of USA

(b) Information Processing Society of Japan
(c) Information Processing Society of Canada
(d) Information Processing Society of India

45. Small group communication generally involves :
(a) 20 persons (b) 40 persons
(c) 29 persons (d) 25 persons

46. In CC-6th edition, the letter 'n' is an ACI, represents which of following?
(a) Serial (b) Critical
(c) Bibliography (d) Biography

47. The classaurus is a vocabulary control tool, developed by Bhattacharya and it is used in :
(a) Indexing language
(b) Post coordinate indexing
(c) Pre Coordinate indexing
(d) None of these

48. What relates the ability of a system not to retrieve non-relevant documents?
(a) Precision (b) Recall
(c) Both (a) and (b) (d) None of these

49. The term "Library Warrant" was first enunciated by :
(a) H.P. Luhn (b) W.A. Katz
(c) 'O' Donal (d) F.W. Hulme

50. The content of 'MARC' record is divided in how many variable fields?
(a) Three (b) Two
(c) Five (d) Six

51. Who was the chairman of National Policy on Library and Information System (NAPLIS)?
(a) S.R. Ranganathan (b) D.P. Chattopadhyay
(c) C.D. Deshmukh (d) Dr. Manmohan Singh

52. Which agency is involved in the production of e-contents under e-PG pathshala programme?
(a) DELNET (b) SIRNET
(c) NICNET (d) INFLIBNET

53. 'E-Shodh Sindhu' e-merged by the merger of :
(a) INFONET (b) INDEST
(c) N-LIST (d) All of these

54. 'N-LIST' programme of 'INFLIBNET' is mainly :
(a) Search Library (b) College Library
(c) Medical Library (d) Law Library

55. The first planner of 'INFLIBNET' was organized in 2003 at :
(a) Ahemadabad (b) Ranchi
(c) Shillong (d) Mumbai

56. First 'CALIBER' of 'INFLIBNET' was organized in 1994 at :
(a) Banglore (b) Pune
(c) Ahamedabad (d) Patna

57. 'CALIBER' 2017 was held at :
(a) B.R.A.B. University, Patna
(b) Banaras Hindu University, U.P.
(c) Jawahar Lal Nehru University, Delhi
(d) Anna University, Chennai

58. 'NICNET' is established in :
(a) India (b) Russia
(c) Japan (d) America

59. Grid System is used in :
(a) Weeding (b) Sampling
(c) Circulation (d) Classification

60. Historical Method of Research is based on :
    (a) Documentary Report
    (b) Survey Report
    (c) Research Tools
    (d) Data Analysis

ANSWERS

1. (c)	2. (a)	3. (b)	4. (d)	5. (b)
6. (a)	7. (b)	8. (b)	9. (d)	10. (b)
11. (a)	12. (c)	13. (a)	14. (b)	15. (c)
16. (a)	17. (c)	18. (b)	19. (a)	20. (d)
21. (b)	22. (a)	23. (d)	24. (b)	25. (c)
26. (a)	27. (c)	28. (b)	29. (c)	30. (a)
31. (a)	32. (c)	33. (b)	34. (b)	35. (d)
36. (b)	37. (d)	38. (b)	39. (a)	40. (c)
41. (a)	42. (c)	43. (d)	44. (b)	45. (d)
46. (a)	47. (c)	48. (a)	49. (d)	50. (b)
51. (b)	52. (d)	53. (d)	54. (b)	55. (c)
56. (c)	57. (d)	58. (a)	59. (b)	60. (a)

Practice Set 25

1. The "Five Law of Library Science" propounded by S.R. Ranganathan, is which types of research?
   (a) Applied Research (b) Pure Research
   (c) Research Survey (d) None of these
2. Whether Library is a System?
   (a) Library is separate form a system
   (b) Yes, it has various sections as sub-systems coordinating each other forming a system
   (c) Both (a) and (b)
   (d) None of these
3. Information Science is a discipline that investigates :
   (a) The means for processing of Information for Optimal Users
   (b) The properties and behaviour of Information
   (c) Both (a) and (b)
   (d) None of these
4. 'KINESIS' is related to :
   (a) Storage (b) Information
   (c) Analysis (d) Communication
5. The term 'BIBLIOPHILE' refers to :
   (a) A author of book (b) A book lover
   (c) A publisher (d) None of these
6. 'MeSH' is the name of a :
   (a) Law Library (b) Medical Library
   (c) CSIR Units (d) None of these

7. Which record is the hub of the stack in a library :
   (a) Book Manual Card (b) Author Register
   (c) Accession Register (d) Shelf List Register

8. 'PLANNER' 2018 was held at :
   (a) Patna University, Patna
   (b) Delhi University, Delhi
   (c) Banaras Hindu University, U.P.
   (d) Tripura University, Agartala

9. "INFLIBNET" Newsletter started its publishing from:
   (a) 2005 (b) 1995
   (c) 2001 (d) 1990

10. Who is responsible for development and maintenance of UGC official website?
    (a) Information Library Network (INFLIBNET)
    (b) National Informetic Centre (NIC)
    (c) Developing Library Network (DELNET)
    (d) None of these

11. 'OJAS' is an initiative of providing facilities to universities and institutions for hosting their journals in open access mode :
    (a) DELNET (b) DRDO
    (c) INFLIBNET (d) CALIBNET

12. 'OJAS' stands for :
    (a) Open Journal Analysis System
    (b) Open Journal Access System
    (c) Open Journal Analytical System
    (d) Open Journal Alphabetical System

13. 'INFOPORT' the subject gateway for Indian Electronic Resources was developed by :
    (a) DELNET (b) NIC
    (c) CALIBNET (d) INFLIBNET

14. 'UGC INFLIBNET' centre is situated at :
    (a) Gandhinagar (b) Mumbai
    (c) Kolkata (d) Chennai
15. Bradford's Law of Scattering is further examined by :
    (a) S.R. Ranganathan (b) H.P. Luhn
    (c) B.C. Vickery (d) 'O' Donal
16. What is the full form of 'RFID'?
    (a) Radio Frequency identification
    (b) Radio Frequency Information Design
    (c) Radio Frequency Infotech Design
    (d) None of these
17. What is the Application of 'RFID' in libraries?
    (a) Book Circulation (b) Stock Verification
    (c) Both (a) and (b) (d) None of these
18. How many ISBN will be given to a book if it is available in four different formats?
    (a) Nine (b) Four
    (c) Two (d) One
19. Who is called father of 'ISBN'?
    (a) Melvil Dewey (b) S.R. Ranganathan
    (c) David Whitaker (d) G. Bhattacharya
20. In which year 13 digit 'ISBN' started?
    (a) 2007 (b) 2005
    (c) 1999 (d) 2010
21. Who developed 10 digit 'ISBN'?
    (a) H.P. Luhn (b) ISO
    (c) S.R. Ranganathan (d) DRDO
22. By which name 'ISO' published the 10 digit ISBN:
    (a) ISO – 2010 (b) ISO – 2016
    (c) ISO – 2018 (d) ISO – 2015

23. In which year ISO published 10 digit 'ISBN'?
    (a) 1979 (b) 1978
    (c) 1950 (d) 1970
24. Which is the 'ISBN' agency in UK?
    (a) National Library of UK
    (b) R.R. Boowker
    (c) The British Library
    (d) None of these
25. In India which is the 'ISBN' agency?
    (a) Raja Ram Mohan Roy Agency
    (b) National Informatic Centre (NIC)
    (c) Information Library Network (INFLIBNET)
    (d) National Library in India
26. How many elements does 'ISBN' number have ?
    (a) Four elements (b) Three elements
    (c) Five elements (d) Six elements
27. How many elements of 'ISBN' have the fixed length?
    (a) Three elements (b) Six elements
    (c) Four elements (d) Two elements
28. How many elements of 'ISBN' can vary in length?
    (a) Three elements (b) Two elements
    (c) One elements (d) Five elements
29. Who is called father of "Indian National Bibliography"?
    (a) S.R. Ranganathan (b) G. Bhattacharya
    (c) B.S. Keshwan (d) K.M. Assaudulah
30. 'EAN' stands for :
    (a) European Analytical Number
    (b) European Article Number

(c) Educational Artistical Number
(d) Educare Article Number

31. An invisible college is a typical example of :
(a) Information Circulation
(b) Information Channel of Communication
(c) Information Retrieval
(d) None of these

32. Berne convention was adopted in the year :
(a) 1898 (b) 1890
(c) 1870 (d) 1886

33. 'FID' was dissolved in the year :
(a) 1995 (b) 2001
(c) 2002 (d) 1990

34. A Gazetteer Information about :
(a) Official Announcements and Notification
(b) Official Records
(c) History of Place
(d) New Library Records

35. The Universal availability of publications (UAP) is a programme launched by :
(a) NISCAIR (b) IFLA
(c) FID (d) DRDO

36. Special Library Association (SLA) was founded in year:
(a) 1925 (b) 1917
(c) 1911 (d) 1909

37. Headquarter of ILA is moved from Calcutta to Delhi in year :
(a) 1972 (b) 1964
(c) 1988 (d) 1960

38. Ranganathan Committee Report on development of university and college libraries was published by :
    (a) University Grant Commission (UGC)
    (b) Raja Ram Mohan Roy Library Foundation (RRRLF)
    (c) Developing Library Network (DELNET)
    (d) Information Library Network (INFLIBNET)
39. Modular Planning of Library Building means :
    (a) Models are build before the final building
    (b) The library is built in stages
    (c) The space is constituted in to modules
    (d) None of these
40. "ATOM INDEX" is brought out by :
    (a) DRTC (b) UNESCO
    (c) MEDLARS (d) INIS
41. "Bibliography of Bibliographies" Comes under :
    (a) Primary Source
    (b) Secondary Source
    (c) Tertiary Source
    (d) Information Communication
42. Citation Indexing was first developed in the field of :
    (a) Literature (b) Law
    (c) Communication (d) Index
43. In which year UBC programme was merged with International MARC programme :
    (a) 1987 (b) 1966
    (c) 1991 (d) 1962
44. Who credited for designing thesaurus :
    (a) Luhn (b) Morle Roget
    (c) M. Taube (d) Neena Brown

45. According to AACR-2, Bhagvad Geeta, Ved and Upanishad are the example of :

(a) Corporate Author (b) Persona Author

(c) Corporate Body (d) None of these

46. The use of 'CD-ROM' in the library significantly relates to which of the following laws?

(a) Fifth Law of Library Science

(b) Second Law of Library Science

(c) Third Law of Library Science

(d) First Law of Library Science

47. Which source would you consult to get the latest information on controversies about the venue for Tata's Nano?

(a) New Dictionary

(b) Annual Reports

(c) India : A Reference Annual

(d) Asian Recorder

48. The quotation "Where is the Wisdom, We Last in Knowledge" is by :

(a) S.R. Ranganathan (b) H.P. Luhn

(c) M. Taube (d) T.S. Eliot

49. 'Entropy' is a measure of :

(a) Degree of uncertainty in Information

(b) Degree of certainty in Information

(c) Both (a) and (b)

(d) None of these

50. In which year was the 'CONPOIS' (India) established:

(a) 1957 (b) 1962

(c) 1975 (d) 1985

51. First time efforts for the development of libraries in India were made :

(a) B.S. Keshwan (b) Mahatma Gandhi
(c) S.R. Ranganathan (d) Sayaji Rao Gaekwad III

52. An e-book which does not require an internet connection to access its contents is :
(a) Digital Book (b) Palm Book
(c) Web Book (d) None of these

53. For fulfilling which law of Library Science, we white class number on catalogue cards by pencil?
(a) First law of library science
(b) Second law of library science
(c) Third law of library science
(d) Fifth law of library science

54. In 2005, Jorge E. Hirsch has suggested it as a tool for Assessing Relative Quality?
(a) R-Index (b) I-Index
(c) H-Index (d) None of these

55. 'Racto' is used for which side of the page of a book?
(a) Left Side (b) Right Side
(c) Middle Side (d) Lower Side

56. Grey Literature generally refers to :
(a) Unpublished literature
(b) Published literature
(c) Private Publication
(d) None of these

57. 'Passive Documentation' means :
(a) Documentation centres
(b) Documentation service
(c) Documentation Development Plane
(d) None of these

58. 'Dublin Core' metadata consist of elements :

(a) 15 elements (b) 14 elements
(c) 16 elements (d) 11 elements

59. Who wrote the book "Manual of Library Economy"?
(a) S.R. Ranganathan (b) Neena Brown
(c) J.D. Brown (d) Melvi Dewey

60. The Information Technology used for simulation of the human thought is known as :
(a) First Information Generation
(b) Second Generation of Computer
(c) Information Communication
(d) Artificial Intellegence

ANSWERS

1. (a)	2. (b)	3. (c)	4. (d)	5. (b)
6. (b)	7. (c)	8. (d)	9. (b)	10. (a)
11. (c)	12. (b)	13. (d)	14. (a)	15. (c)
16. (a)	17. (c)	18. (b)	19. (c)	20. (a)
21. (b)	22. (c)	23. (d)	24. (b)	25. (a)
26. (c)	27. (d)	28. (a)	29. (c)	30. (b)
31. (b)	32. (d)	33. (c)	34. (a)	35. (b)
36. (d)	37. (b)	38. (a)	39. (c)	40. (d)
41. (c)	42. (b)	43. (a)	44. (b)	45. (d)
46. (a)	47. (c)	48. (d)	49. (a)	50. (d)
51. (d)	52. (a)	53. (d)	54. (c)	55. (b)
56. (a)	57. (b)	58. (a)	59. (c)	60. (d)